LOST,
STOLEN *or*
SHREDDED

LOST, STOLEN *or* SHREDDED

Stories of Missing Works
of Art and Literature

RICK GEKOSKI

P

PROFILE BOOKS

Published in Great Britain in 2013 by
PROFILE BOOKS LTD
3A Exmouth House
Pine Street
Exmouth Market
London EC1R 0JH
www.profilebooks.com

10 9 8 7 6 5 4 3 2 1

Extract from 'Sage Homme' by Ezra Pound, from *Selected Letters 1907–1941 of Ezra Pound*, copyright ©1950 by Ezra Pound. Reprinted by permission of New Directions Publishing Corp., and © Estate of Ezra Pound and reprinted by permission of Faber and Faber Ltd
Extract from 'Aubade' © Estate of Philip Larkin and reprinted by permission of Faber and Faber Ltd
Extract from 'How to Win the Next Election' © Estate of Philip Larkin and reprinted by permission of Faber and Faber Ltd

Typeset in Sabon by MacGuru Ltd
info@macguru.org.uk

Printed and bound in Great Britain by
Clays, Bungay, Suffolk

A CIP catalogue record for this book is available from the British Library.

ISBN 978 1 84668 491 3
eISBN 978 1 84765 932 3

The paper this book is printed on is certified by the © 1996 Forest Stewardship Council A.C. (FSC). It is ancient-forest friendly. The printer holds FSC chain of custody SGS-COC-2061

FSC
www.fsc.org
MIX
Paper from
responsible sources
FSC® C018072

For Steve Broome

Contents

Foreword

He collected absences. For him they were more intense, vibrant and real than the presences that they shadowed. And this one – he'd just heard the news of the most audacious art theft of his time – was astonishing, quite enough to merit a change of travel plans. And so he and his friend Max departed from Milan and headed for Paris, the scene of the crime.

On a day early in September 1911 they arrived at the Louvre that little bit late to join the queue, heightening the anticipation. When they eventually entered the Salon Carré, they approached the spot where the *Mona Lisa* had been displayed for generations. The crowd – all of whom had come on the same pilgrimage – pushed forward, and the little man, jostled, could hardly see. Taking his friend by the shoulder, Max pushed to the very front. Other onlookers paused to deposit flowers on the floor beneath, with notes of remembrance tied in silk ribbons.

He stood in front of the wall, those obsidian eyes staring, rapt. The painting was gone. That's why he was there. It had been stolen a week before, and the Museum had only just reopened to the public. The crowd had come expressly to see where it used to be, and now wasn't.

For Franz Kafka, the absent *Mona Lisa* was in the process of joining the internal collection that he called his 'invisible curiosities': sights, monuments and works of art that he had missed seeing. The phrase, like many of Kafka's aperçus, is both puzzling and provocative. It occurs several times in his writing, often in the context of thinking about the movies. Max Brod refers to the idea (it is unclear which of them first used it) in describing a scene in a film in which a young woman is travelling quickly in a taxi at night in Munich: 'We see, of all edifices, only the first floor, since the car's big visor blocks our view. Fantastic imaginings of the height of the palaces and churches.'

Kafka, musing on the scene and imaginatively engaged by what is not seen, expanded the image, as the 'driver calls out the names of the invisible sights'. What fascinates him is that something significant is out there, moving by too quickly to apprehend, as in a few seconds' exposure in a film.

Travelling on hissing tires, in the back of a taxi on a rainy night, a cityscape partially revealed as it whizzes by, might be taken as a metaphor for the human journey. A concentrated act of attention, peering out the window, can only frustrate, with its suggestions of larger hidden presences. What is imperfectly revealed is a shadowy simulacrum of what is most assuredly out there, if only one had the light, the time and the right vantage point from which to see it.

There is a similarity between this image and that of Plato's allegory of the caves, in which a fully realised world casts its shadow on the wall, and is taken to be all that there is. In Kafka's reframing of the metaphor, though, there is a doubly troubling centre: again there is the blurred approximation of the real, but in the taxi image the onlooker is aware of his estrangement from that fleeting world, whereas in Plato's the shadows are taken to be all that there is.

So: are we all tootling about in taxis, craning our necks at the unlit streets? Not at all; you don't always take a cab. What we have here – which is so typical of Kafka – is a suggestive moment which seems to have some general application, but also resists it. There are plenty of experiences in which we walk the streets in the presence of the familiar: buildings, people, landscapes, seen in clear light. Kafka, though, is more imaginatively engaged by the barely apprehended, suggestive, lost. There is, after all, something wearying, predictable and banal, about knowing things.

This fascination with what is shimmeringly and incompletely present haunts Kafka's imagination and pervades his work. He is the perfect onlooker for an absent presence, not for the *Mona Lisa* itself but for where it used to be. She had been stolen, or perhaps one should say kidnapped? But why such a crowd? More people had come to see where the *Mona Lisa* used to be than had attended when it was hanging in its accustomed place. What were they looking at, and for? Because all they saw was a shadowy band of grime on the wall that marked the outlines of the missing picture, and which seemed in itself to frame the possibilities of new imagining. Could the assembled throng – they knew the image, most of them – project it into that seemingly empty space? For the moment it almost made artists of them.

I have invoked the figure of Franz Kafka, queuing excitedly to add to his catalogue of absences, not because there is something surreal – something Kafkaesque – in his pursuit, but because he is, for once, typical. There is nothing eccentric in his obsession with absent objects and lost opportunities. Kafka stands, here, both for myself and, I hope, for my reader. We are all curious about our invisible curiosities.

Lost, Stolen or Shredded consists of a series of chapters broadly based on stories of lost works of art and literature, where 'lost' means, as Humpty Dumpty remarked firmly about his choice of a word, 'just what I choose it to mean'. They can be read individually, for it is not my aim to write generally about the nature of loss, or to give some potted history of works of art that have been lost. No fun in that.

When a wilful destruction of a work is contemplated, knotty moral problems may attend the act. Was Philip Larkin's secretary right to shred his diaries, shortly before his death? Or Byron's executors to burn his *Memoirs*? Was Max Brod right to reject Kafka's final instruction to burn all of his unpublished manuscripts?

For me, the stories of Byron, Larkin and Kafka are connected to each other, mutually illuminate, force distinction and discrimination, both confuse and illustrate, lead inevitably to philosophical, moral and psychological reflection. Stories of loss attach to each other like stray atoms, coagulate and grow into something more complex and more compelling than single entities.

If you want to understand the attachment engendered by works of art, you would do better to read Bruce Chatwin's *Utz*, or Henry James's *The Spoils of Poynton*, than a treatise on the subject. We often learn more from a compelling story than from whole volumes of sociology or art history. Stories are more entertaining, more instructive, and more memorable. They stick in the mind, and to each other: they make a world.

These stories are chosen because they are part of my own internal museum of loss. In recounting them I am, inevitably, also writing about myself. All writing, admittedly, is a form of autobiography, however impersonal and 'objective' it may seem. The way in which we see and value things, put them together, express their meanings and relations, inevitably reveals something of the mind and voice of the observer, whether they be a novelist or a mathematician. Wordsworth observes that the world as we encounter it is something that we 'half perceive and half create', and I have felt it necessary in writing these chapters, which are part essay and part memoir, to reveal and to interrogate both elements of this process. What is out there? Why, and how, do I care?

In the course of the forthcoming chapters I occasionally seem to find myself on both sides of a question, apparently unable or unwilling to choose, so complex and intractable are the questions. There's danger in this, to be sure. It seems to offer a soft option, to absolve one from thinking sufficiently hard about a topic finally to come down on one side or the other.

Is it regrettable that cultural objects are forcibly appropriated from their native soil and transported to foreign museums? Yes. Is it a boon and a delight that we can visit those museums and learn about other civilisations? Certainly.

Can it be right to destroy an important work of art, as Winston Churchill's wife burned a portrait of him by Graham Sutherland? It seems a vile precedent, which gives credibility to the enemies of culture such as the Maoists, with their wholesale conflagration of centuries of Chinese art, architecture and literature. And yet there are instances – is this one? – in which such vandalism seems justifiable.

It's easy enough to scrape away at such tensions, smooth them over, force the recalcitrant material into easier shapes. That is just what I have tried to avoid. Anyone who is not perplexed by the complex issues surrounding the loss of works of art hasn't thought about them sufficiently.

There is a phrase in Joseph Conrad's *Heart of Darkness* that is apposite here. Trying desperately to understand the full implications of what has happened to him on his appalling trip down the Congo, the narrator muses that 'the meaning of an episode was not inside like a kernel but outside, enveloping the tale which brought it out only as a glow brings out a haze'. Though this has caused one commentator to accuse the author of 'making a virtue out of not knowing what he means', I'm on Conrad's side on this one. I distrust people who emphatically know what they mean.

I rather like that haziness, with its suggestion that when we seek to understand our most complex 'episodes' it is only by craning our necks, squinting our eyes, trying to make out what is imperfectly before us. Like Kafka and Max Brod in that night-time taxi ride, trying to perceive what is only partially knowable. When we are faced with ultimate questions and intractable mysteries, meaning is often imperfectly apprehended, guessed at rather than mastered, tantalisingly ungraspable: a glow that brings out a haze.

It's a most elusive metaphor, dangerous in its way, a counsel to accept ambiguity and clearly to honour unclarity: to provide a sense of the world, of its muddle and unseen presences, that is accurate and moving, provocative, real.

1

Has Anyone Seen the *Mona Lisa*?

When I attended Huntington High School, in Long Island, in the late 1950s we had a neighbour, who lived five houses down to the right if you faced our (identical) house, named Mr Andrews. He was distinguished and rather pompous, with a fruity modulated voice – perhaps he was English, or wished to be? – always formally dressed and with immaculately cut, wavy grey hair, which he wore rather longer than most gentlemen of the time, presumably as a sign of his artistic nature. Recently retired from the law, he now spent much of his time painting in oils. He was, he regularly affirmed, extremely good at it, particularly at making copies of famous paintings. So good, in fact, that apparently 'the best curators at the Met' were unable, on the basis of visual evidence alone, to distinguish an Andrews from a Da Vinci: his version of the *Mona Lisa*, he chortled, had fooled them entirely.

I didn't believe him, but there was something so audacious in the claim that a tiny sliver of doubt remained in my mind. I looked carefully at his copy of the picture, which hung over his brick fireplace, like my parents' (palpable) reproduction of Renoir's *The Boating Party*. It looked pretty good to me. I was fifteen at the time, and I'd grown up on such reproductions.

When I was a boy, I loved going to museum shops. In the galleries themselves I would rush about, seeking a picture or image that I wanted to take home. In the shop afterwards I would systematically go through the available reproductions to see if I could find my favourite to put on my bedroom wall. At six I wanted a soft-focus Rembrandt image of a seated woman – my mother never sat still, and was certainly not soft-focus – but it was soon replaced by an Alexander Calder print in orange and blue, and that a year or two later by a perky Miró. I could not bear the idea that my pictures should hang (as it were) side by side: Miró replaced Calder, he didn't join him. This process continued for a surprisingly long time, as if just one image were quite sufficient by way of self-definition. In my dorm at Penn I had a poster of that Picasso dove, and a few years later my rather spare room in Merton College, Oxford, had a blue-period Picasso nude as its only adornment. I didn't give up this habit until I had to, when renting my first flat gave me such wall space that it demanded filling. It was rather fun, spreading things out, putting things together.

It was only in my thirties that I began to abjure copies in favour of originals. My parents' *The Boating Party* looked pretty much real, aside from the fact that it wasn't. You could fill a room with similarly good reproductions of the finest paintings, and I have no doubt that they would look terrific to an ignorant eye. But such reproductions were, I began to feel, vulgar and undesirable.

Mr Andrews's Mona Lisa image was certainly intended, in a playful manner, to deceive, but it was not a forgery, simply a copy. The forger Mark Hofmann, whose copies of Mormon letters and the *Oath of a Freeman* were presented

Who stole the *Mona Lisa*? Clue: look at the four iron pegs.

as 'discoveries', intended to profit through his capacity to deceive the experts, whereas Mr Andrews's modest home industry was a harmless hobby, and his capacity to fool all those curators was merely a source of pride and amusement to him, not a source of income. No doubt the inflation of his self-worth was a by-product of the process, even more irritating to his wife and children, I suspect, than to us neighbours. Or maybe they were proud of him? After all, Mr Andrews was in a long tradition of copyists of Da Vinci's masterpiece, dating back to the time of Leonardo's production of the picture in the early sixteenth century.

A strikingly fine copy of the *Mona Lisa* has been owned by Madrid's Prado Museum since it opened in 1819, which can pretty reliably be described as contemporary to the real thing, likely enough to have emanated from one of the assistants at the Master's own studios. It is painted on a small walnut panel, an expensive material which had been used by Leonardo for several paintings, including *The Lady with an Ermine* (1490) and *St John the Baptist* (1516), and it may well have been commissioned by a wealthy buyer frustrated by his inability to get Leonardo to sell the real thing.

There are apparently dozens of copies of the picture dating from the sixteenth and seventeenth centuries, though no one knows how many of these were simply acts of homage (which was common at the time) and how many were intended to pass profitably as the *Mona Lisa* itself: the essential difference between a copy and a fake. Most of these surviving versions are distinctly inferior to the real thing and unlikely ever to be confused with it, even by a fifteen-year-old. But for so many copies to have been produced so quickly after the original composition seems odd – can they all have worked from the King of France's original? – and suggests, at least, that there was more than one version to copy.

The Prado version, if it did emanate from Leonardo's workshop, may well have served as a second model. Ironically, that copy, though certainly distinguishable from the real thing to an expert eye, is a work of great beauty which is more accessible than Leonardo's own picture, having recently undergone two years of restoration, which have cleared layers of black paint overlay to reveal details of the background that are now obscure in the original. Leonardo's picture has never been restored by the Louvre, because the many layers of cracked varnish make it too risky a process with such a fragile surface.

The result, if you look at the pictures side by side (they were exhibited together, for the first time, at the Louvre in March 2012), is that the studio copy is much clearer and gives a much better idea of the original composition. On the left of La Gioconda's head, the craggy landscape is crisp, with the details of the grey rock formations absolutely precise. In comparison, this whole area in the original is much darker and obscure in detail.

But even if the Louvre version had been restored, and (let us surmise) the two pictures were now well nigh indistinguishable, the Leonardo would still be entitled to the greater respect and admiration, for his picture carries with it the facts of its composition and can be traced to his own hand. What we have now are two competing versions, one restored to what it may originally have looked like in the early sixteenth century, the other bearing all too obviously the effects of time upon a painted surface. I greatly prefer the latter, not just because it is the original, but because I like what time does to things, how ageing deepens and shadows, produces a glow of its own. Patination is why we admire seventeenth-century oak cupboards, respond so deeply to the depth and glow that the wood acquires over the centuries. Our response to the *Mona Lisa* in the Louvre, its eerie and unexpected combination of filminess and the sharp reality that throws her smile into such enigmatic relief, is the effect of the years upon the surface of the paint, so that the sitter seems to emerge from the depths of a shimmering timelessness.

We speak too frequently of the ravages of time and too little of the glow that it can produce. The villa of Calpurnius Piso, which was destroyed in the eruption of Vesuvius, and which housed one of the finest libraries of Classical antiquity, provided the model for the first Getty Museum, which opened in 1974. I visited the museum in 2006, just after a major renovation from its original incarnation, and hated it at first sight. No patination, no gravitas. Kapow! So bright and new, the reds fresh as the day they came out of the can, the yellows too insistent, released from the effects of time. The effect was startling, unsettling and unpleasant. So many bright colours, so many new statues, rooms, fountains, courtyards. It looked like a well-designed McMansion, vulgar and self-important. Nouveau Riche. I yearned to experience it in its old age, tired, ruined, Roman! Lacking antiquity, spared both the enhancements and the ravages of time, it simply looked like a house that one would never – no matter how much money one had – build for oneself, or even consent to visit, unless one were a Roman, way back then.

The Getty villa is not a restoration but a replica, and rather less successful than some other attempts to recreate the past, such as the shockingly beautiful Ishtar Gate at Berlin's Pergamon Museum, which was partly built with materials excavated from the original site. Yet restoration provides us with an analogous set of problems to replication, for if the restorer attempts to return an object to its original state (a topic much in dispute in the profession), they are in danger of making something old look, simply, as if it were new. There was ferocious criticism in 1994, when an over-zealous cleansing of Michelangelo's decorations to the ceiling of the Sistine Chapel produced a result so fresh that many people felt that, if the grimy encrustation of time had been stripped from the surfaces, so had the gravitas. The result could have been recently painted by my old neighbour Mr Andrews, if he'd been as talented as he claimed.

And so, alas and rather shamingly, it was him of whom I was thinking on my first visit to the Louvre in 1963, as I approached the *Mona Lisa*. It was hard to get a proper look at it, but from the few bits I could discern it was clearly better than the version that fooled all those curators, in Mr Andrews's living room. On later visits to Paris, in the late 1960s, during my years at Oxford, I always made it a point to pop into the Louvre to revisit the *Mona Lisa*, as if dropping in on a friend. Drawn, in the first instances, by the painting's mystique – the most famous painting in the world! That enigmatic smile, that inimitably captivating presence! – I later came to be more interested in the crowds surrounding it than in the picture itself. These were then stereotyped as 'camera-laden Japanese tourists', but you weren't allowed to take pictures, and only a small percentage of the visitors were Japanese anyway.

It didn't matter where you were from, the behaviour was exactly the same: spectators rising on tiptoes, craning their necks, trying to get a glimpse of her Mona-ness. What these frustrated viewers had in common was simple. Desperate to view they might have been, but few of them seemed to know a damn thing about art. Art wasn't the point. She, herself, that smiling icon, she was the point. The gathered throng had come not to see a painting, but to peer at a celebrity: they were aesthetic paparazzi. The only tragedy was that you were not allowed to get your camera out. What a missed opportunity! To have one's picture taken with such a lady!

The history of the painting is a little obscure, but it most likely dates from Leonardo's residence in Florence between 1503 and 1505. Even by contemporary standards the picture was technically remarkable for its use of sfumato, by which the background dissolves in form, giving a mysterious blending of light and shade, and an unearthly timelessness. Leonardo achieved this effect, according to recent research at the Centre de Recherche et de Restauration des Musées de France, by applying over forty layers – probably using his fingers rather than a brush – of thin glaze. If you mix this with various pigments, you will eventually get the blurry shadowy quality that can be observed round the Mona Lisa's mouth, and that evanescent smile which seems to come and go: an uncommon example of a smile being wiped not off but onto someone's face. According to the researcher Philippe Walter, 'even today, Leonardo's realisation of such a thin layer remains an amazing feat.'

Yet the smile for which the lady was to become famous did not strike its first onlookers as remarkable. A contemporary manual describing the correct deportment of young ladies recommends just such a look: 'close the mouth at the right corner with a suave and nimble movement', it advises, 'and open it on the left side, as if you were smiling secretly.' Some years later, Leonardo was to use a similar smile on the faces of his pictures of St Anne (1510) and St John (1516), both of which also hang in the Louvre. Curiously, that expression seems to fit the face of women and men equally well. In fact, a number of commentators, both ancient and modern, have maintained that the reason for La Gioconda's apparent bemusement is that she is actually a self-portrait of the artist in drag – which a computer expert in 1997 claimed he could prove by almost seamlessly superimposing Leonardo's face over that of his supposed subject.

Perhaps this is why Leonardo loved the picture so much that he couldn't bear to relinquish it. He travelled with her as with a mistress – he couldn't keep his hands off her – until, some time in the 1530s, he sold the painting to François I for the enormous sum of about $100,000 in today's money. From that time the portrait was the possession of the kings of France until it was deposited in the Louvre early in the eighteenth century. It became an immediate favourite at the new gallery, and its fame grew as the century progressed.

On the morning of 21 August 1911 the Louvre was closed, as it always was on Mondays. Nevertheless, a staff of over 800 people might be found within the building's massive confines: the museum covers over 49 acres and houses half a million works of art. Some time between 7.00 and 8.30 in the morning – while one of the attendants went for coffee and another was sleeping – someone walked into the Salon Carré, took the *Mona Lisa* off the wall and vanished. Its absence was noted within the hour, but it was assumed that the painting had been taken to be photographed. As the hours passed, its absence was increasingly remarked: 'Has anyone seen the *Mona Lisa*?' First curiously, then anxiously, then frantically, the question was repeated during the course of the day. Where was it? No, it wasn't being photographed, nor had it been removed for conservation or cleaning, nor were there plans to reframe or rehang it. There was no reason for it not to be there. 'Has anyone seen the *Mona Lisa*?'

Many hours passed before the unthinkable was confirmed. The picture's frame was found in a stairwell, but the lady herself had vanished. 'It was as if someone had stolen one of the towers of Notre Dame', said the museum's Director, Théophile Homolle, as if to suggest that the painting had been equally securely in its place. It hadn't been: security at the Louvre was so lax, and objects disappeared with such frequency, that it was mildly surprising that anything was left there at all.

On Tuesday morning sixty police officers were dispatched, art lovers coming out of the Louvre were searched, railway stations were patrolled. But it was too late; the thief had had too long to get away. Where did he go? Where did she? Who took her? Reports in the newspapers treated the case as an abduction, or a kidnapping, rather than a mere theft.

The police and public were desperate for a quick arrest. Rumours flew about. The picture had been stolen to blackmail the government! Perhaps by a gang! That would do it. And some sort of conspiracy too. An informant calling himself Baron Ignace d'Ormesson approached the *Paris-Journal* newspaper with a story of how, four years earlier, he had regularly stolen objects from the Louvre's Asiatic

Antiquities section, and then sold them to various people in Paris. It was easy, he said, as long as the object wasn't too big. Prompted to do it again, he quickly produced (for a price of 250 francs) a newly pilfered object, which was displayed in the newspaper's office. Crowds flocked to see it. Presumably this (now vanished) baron, if he could be apprehended, was also responsible for the theft of the *Mona Lisa*?

Perhaps – the speculation was distinctly flimsy – this baron was connected to that band of radical artists who wished to overthrow the established order? It was a time of revolutionary anarchism, both ineffectual and murderous, and extreme opinions were relentlessly à la mode, like the latest frocks. The poet Guillaume Apollinaire, for instance, adamantly insisted that all museums had to be destroyed, as the old made way for a new world of imagining. He and his friend Pablo Picasso, who held similar opinions, signed a manifesto pledging to burn down the Louvre. Why not? They were advocates of Marinetti's Futurist Manifesto of 1909, which was unambiguous in its revolutionary rhetoric:

> We are issuing this manifesto of ruinous and incendiary violence, by which we today are founding Futurism, because we want to deliver Italy from its gangrene of professors, archaeologists, tourist guides and antiquaries.
>
> Italy has been too long the great second-hand market. We want to get rid of the innumerable museums which cover it with innumerable cemeteries.

The threatened violence is, of course, metaphorical at best, largely fatuous bombast, but easily mistaken for something more dangerous. Bombs, after all, were being detonated. The

Royal Observatory in Greenwich had been bombed in 1894 (prompting Conrad's 1907 novel *The Secret Agent*): if these lunatics could attack the very site and idea of Time, surely they could attempt to destroy Art and History as well?

The police rarely read anarchist manifestos as symbolic and aesthetic statements, and they were right not to do so. How does one distinguish a bunch of artists fuelled by revolutionary fervour from a band of anarchists genuinely determined to blow things up? The period between 1880 and the start of the First World War was one of terrifying and widespread anarchist activity. Real bombs, real stabbings, real death. Anarchist attacks occurred in sixteen countries, and (excluding Russia, which is almost a story on its own) over 500 people were killed worldwide.

La bande à Picasso – or the Wild Men of Paris, as they were sometimes known – were perfect suspects: what better than to steal the painting and hold it for some sort of ransom? What sort? Who knows? No one was thinking very clearly. It was time for an arrest!

Picasso was particularly vulnerable, for he had been the purchaser of some statuettes stolen from the Louvre, which could be found in his flat in the Boulevard de Clichy. Rushing back from Céret, where he had been painting in the French Pyrenees, he was met at the railway station by the terrified Apollinaire, whose flat had recently been raided by the police. If Picasso's was similarly investigated, the presence of the two statuettes, each bearing the Louvre's ownership stamp, would have been unambiguously incriminating. They had been purchased from the elusive Baron d'Ormesson, and there is good reason to suppose that they may have been stolen to order. The two pieces – Bronze

Age statuettes from Spain of a man and a woman carved in stone – had provided inspiration for Picasso's revolutionary painting *Les Demoiselles d'Avignon* (1907). Aware that he was perilously at risk, Picasso bundled them into a suitcase and made a midnight visit to the Seine, criss-crossing the roads to avoid being followed. But he couldn't force himself to destroy the works and returned to his flat disconsolate, with the damning evidence still in his possession.

Some nineteen days after the theft of the *Mona Lisa*, the painter was interviewed in his studio by the gendarmerie, and summoned to appear before a magistrate on the charge of receiving art stolen from the Louvre, though (curiously) the detectives did not search the premises in search of it. Picasso was terrified. In the courtroom he met a distraught and dishevelled Apollinaire, who had already spent two days in jail. Apollinaire had already confessed to everything and anything proposed to him by the police, implicating Picasso in the purchase of the two statuettes.

'And what do you have to say to this?' the Magistrate demanded of Picasso.

Picasso wept, begged forgiveness, denied everything, including any acquaintance with Apollinaire. Eventually released on his own recognisance but banned from leaving Paris, Picasso was allowed to return home, where he lived in a state of high anxiety for some months. A few days later Apollinaire was freed from jail – the lack of any evidence implicating him had proven something of an obstacle – and he was later to call it 'strange, incredible, tragic and amusing' that he was the only person in France ever arrested for the theft of the *Mona Lisa*.

When the Louvre reopened, a week following the theft,

thousands of people – including Franz Kafka and Max Brod – queued for hours to enter the Salon Carré simply to gaze at the empty space where the *Mona Lisa* had hung. It was enough to make a French philosopher – a Sartre or a Lacan (who, curiously, was later Picasso's doctor) – swoon with delight. If Mona Lisa had been a compelling presence, she was even more fascinating in her absence. (As Gertrude Stein observed in a different context, it was a time when paintings were trying to escape from their frames.)

The newspapers were ferociously critical: the French love blaming. The Director of the Louvre and the chief attendant were fired. Hoaxes were posited, suspicious eyes were cast on the Germans. Alphonse Bertillon, who had recently invented a method of fingerprint identification, was called in, and lifted a beauty from the abandoned frame. Unfortunately he couldn't match it to any of those he had on file (it came from the wrong thumb).

In fact, it didn't take a Sherlock Holmes – hardly even an Inspector Clouseau – to figure out the first place to look. If the lady had been snatched, it had to have been done quickly, and only an expert could have done that. The *Mona Lisa* had been mounted on the wall using four iron pegs. If you knew how to do it, the picture came off in a matter of seconds. But (as police attempts to remove a picture clumsily demonstrated), if you didn't know the trick, it could take two men up to five minutes. Where to look? It was almost certainly an inside job. How about one of the people who had re-installed the picture only a year earlier?

Vincenzo Peruggia, an itinerant Italian picture framer, had been one of the team who were responsible for the picture's re-hanging. He was interviewed, but (unlike the

Director of the Louvre) he was never fingerprinted. Why should he be? Everyone agreed the painting had been taken by a criminal mastermind, either stolen on behalf of a reclusive and ruthless American millionaire or held to ransom. Or maybe it was one of those dratted anarchists.

In fact, though, it was the unprepossessing Italian who had walked unobserved into the gallery, taken the picture and removed it from its frame, and strolled out with it hidden under the white smock worn by many of the museum staff. For over two years the *Mona Lisa* languished in her lover's squalid bed-sitting room before Peruggia, his passion slaked, decided it was time for her to go home.

It was at this point, I suspect, that he concocted the story that was to make him a national hero. Single-handedly, he claimed, he had performed a patriotic act: he was returning the *Mona Lisa* to Italy, from which (he wrongly believed) she had been taken by the vile Napoleon. Ignorant of the possible avenues for selling stolen pictures, Peruggia wrote to a leading art dealer in Florence, Alfredo Geri, who had recently advertised for old pictures. Signing his letter 'Leonardo', the thief offered the *Mona Lisa*, suggesting that Geri come to Paris to view the painting, for which he was asking 100,000 francs (ironically, roughly identical to its price in the 1530s).

All dealers get a host of apparently cranky letters, and mostly we throw them away. Geri almost did so too, until an obscure intuition made him pause. After all, the lady was out there somewhere ... He enticed Peruggia and his consort to Florence, arguing plausibly that the Director of the Uffizi needed to verify the authenticity of the picture before he could proceed with the purchase. On Wednesday,

17 November 1913, Geri and Giovanni Poggi went to 'Leonardo's' modest hotel room, where (in Geri's words):

> He locked the door and drew out from under his bed a trunk of white wood that was full of wretched objects: broken shoes, a mangled hat, a pair of pliers, plastering tools, a smock, some paint brushes, and even a mandolin. Then, from under a false bottom in the box he took out an object wrapped in red silk … and to our astonished eyes the divine 'Gioconda' appeared, intact and marvellously preserved.

There was no doubt about authenticity: the picture still bore on its reverse the identifying marks from the Louvre. They inspected the picture minutely, admired it extravagantly and called the police.

At the subsequent trial in Italy, Peruggia vehemently protested his innocence, maintaining that he had acted from altruistic motives. (The 100,000 franc asking price was presumably to cover his expenses.) He was sent to jail for the remarkably short period of seven months, during which time he was treated as a national hero. So many gifts, cheques, flowers, titbits of food, sacks of coffee and boxes of chocolate arrived that he had to be moved to a larger cell.

The theft of the *Mona Lisa*, and its repatriation, was claimed as an altruistic act, though this was nonsense. Peruggia stole the picture to make money, just as Leonardo had parted with it for the same reason. But the public response to Peruggia's justification for the theft was revealing, and funny. For however brief a moment, the *Mona Lisa* had come home, and throngs of people were as delighted as Greeks might be upon the return of the Elgin Marbles.

But it could not last, and the *Mona Lisa* soon made her slow way back to her adoptive home, stopping at a museum or two on the way to elicit the admiration of tens of thousands of Italians. Crowds arrived at the railway stations through which she travelled, hoping to catch a final glimpse of the lady. If she was leaving Italy for the last time, at least one could say goodbye, maybe take a picture. The assembled throng was largely silent and reverent, and one cannot avoid juxtaposing the image, almost a century later, of Princess Diana's body being carried up the motorway to her resting place on the island at Althorp, as mournful crowds wished her a good final journey.

In the view of the Director of the Uffizi, she had never been stolen, nor even kidnapped. His view was that she had eloped, and tried to come home. She always was a devious lady: surely that tricky Renaissance smile tells you that. Indeed, Peruggia, in one of the various and contradictory stories that he gave with regard to his motives, claimed that he had gone into the Louvre to steal some other painting, but that as he passed her the Lady smiled seductively at him. Take me! Perhaps she fancied him? Or was she merely looking for a way out? Women chained to uncongenial destinies often choose odd bedfellows to make their escape.

2

Possession and Dispossession in New Zealand: The Theft of the Urewera Mural

Lake Waikaremoana is unknown to most visitors to New Zealand, who are more likely to be drawn by obvious and accessible sites, by Lake Taupo, Hawkes Bay, Milford Sound or the Bay of Islands. New Zealanders are quietly pleased by this, and like to regard this isolated spot in the Urewera National Park as a secret, and a treasure. (The web site describes the lake as 'New Zealand's Best Kept Secret'.) The lakeside facilities are rudimentary, which Kiwis also like, though there is – or was – a Visitors' Centre, a campsite and a few chalets for rent, which are all primary colours, unpretentious building materials and acute angles, comfortable enough for a few nights by the water. The effect of the buildings is smart, simple and quietly memorable, characteristic hallmarks of the work of the highly regarded Maori architect John Scott.

When I first stayed at the lake, I was immediately struck – silenced almost – by the eerie quiet, the unexpected psychic weight of the place. No sounds of souped-up motor boats or jet skis on the lake – they are forbidden – but hardly any sounds of people either. Even the children of visitors are hushed, as if acceding to some ancient imperative that issues from deep within the landscape. Round the lake, native bush – the Kiwi name for the indigenous forest – rises, and is reflected in the waters as an ebony sheen. Dark green, black. It is a sombre place, with a quiet gravitas that speaks to something deep in the national consciousness.

The site is administered by the Department of Conservation, though the John Scott-designed Visitors' Centre is now closed and has been replaced by a temporary building. The major display at the original Centre, the modest facade of which did not hint at the treat to come, was an immense (18 × 5½ feet) painting on canvas by Colin McCahon – 'the Urewera mural' – which dominated the interior with its sombre imagery. Black, mostly black. Bit of dark green too, and a few ochre notes for the painted inscriptions, for which the artist was famous. McCahon was already recognised as New Zealand's greatest artist when the painting was commissioned in 1975 to hang in the newly built Centre. The painter was asked to portray 'the mystery of man in the Urewera', and the result has come to be regarded, for reasons both of its intrinsic quality and its remarkable history, as New Zealand's most famous painting. When I first saw it, it seemed overwhelmingly to catch the spirit of the place, and though its complex political implications were lost on me, the mural had a satisfying authority that spoke of serious matters, seriously addressed.

From its very first appearance it had been a controversial picture, which offended the complex and often contradictory local sensibilities both by what it said and by what it left out. To understand the depth of feeling involved, you need

'It's a painful love, loving a land': Colin McCahon's Urewera Mural.

to know something of the history of the region and of the dispossession of the Tuhoe ('People of the Mist'), who have lived there for centuries before the coming of the Pakeha, or European settlers.

New Zealand's founding document is the Treaty of Waitangi between the British Crown and Maori. The rangitira (or chiefs) of most Maori tribes signed the treaty as copies were carted round the country in 1840. Most significantly, however, the Tuhoe did not sign, and were in fact not offered the opportunity.

The Colonial Secretary's intentions leading to the Treaty were both clear and honourable:

> All dealings with the Aborigines for their Lands must be conducted on the same principles of sincerity, justice, and good faith as must govern your transactions with them for the recognition of Her Majesty's Sovereignty in the Islands. Nor is this all. They must not be permitted to enter into any Contracts in which they might be the ignorant and unintentional authors of injuries to themselves. You will not, for example, purchase from them any Territory the retention of which by them would be essential, or highly conducive, to their own comfort, safety or subsistence. The acquisition of Land by the Crown for the future Settlement of British Subjects must be confined to such Districts as the Natives can alienate without distress or serious inconvenience to themselves. To secure the observance of this rule will be one of the first duties of their official protector.

Sadly, it didn't work straight away. For about thirty years, from 1843, a series of brutal wars were waged, increasingly alienating laws were passed, and punitive land confiscations were made, to assist the new European immigrants flooding the country in search of land.

Fast forward to the present, and the lasting grievances of Maori relating to the Treaty are subject to an ongoing forensic examination by the Waitangi Tribunal, established in 1975, the longevity and complexity of whose deliberations make Kafka's jurists in *The Trial* look simple and expeditious souls. The Tribunal has issued two massive reports into claims relating to the Urewera region, and the Tuhoe are in the process of attempting to negotiate a settlement that they hope will include the restoration to them of 212,000 hectares of land within the Urewera National Park, which is certainly a highly contentious claim.

The Tribunal was unequivocal:

The report also examines the confiscation of Tuhoe land in the 1860s by the Crown. The confiscation was designed to punish other iwi [tribes] but it also included much of Tuhoe's best land. No land was ever returned to Tuhoe, even though the Crown had not intended to punish them. Largely in response to this, some Te Urewera iwi supported Te Kooti in attacks on Mohaka and other places in 1869, with about 80 Maori and Pakeha being killed. The Crown responded by sending an armed force into Te Urewera, killing non-combatants and destroying homes, food supplies, and taonga. Many people died, either as casualties or from hunger and disease, and this created a lasting legacy of pain and grievance.

The Tuhoe have continued to suffer, many of them feel, the disenfranchisement of an occupied people, the deprivation and loss of cultural identity. They are not, they claim, New Zealanders, and many yearn for the creation of a separate Tuhoe nation.

McCahon's mural makes explicit reference to these events and aspirations, and incorporates references to Tuhoe history and mythology. But the wording of the first version of his painted inscription had been controversial, and various alterations which in the artist's view would 'glorify' the Tuhoe were suggested and rejected. Though sympathetic to the Tuhoe cause, McCahon was reluctant to accept multiple changes of wording which would affect not merely the meaning of the inscription but the formal balance of the painting itself. After almost a year of negotiation with the Urewera National Park Board, McCahon announced he was withdrawing the picture and would sell it through the art trade instead. He first offered to create a replacement mural with the revised wording, but eventually concurred and made the minimal suggested changes: 'It's not a replacement but a rewrite ... a bit messy as I guessed it would be but it should be okay.' After over a year of negotiations, the picture was at last in the right place for more or less the right reasons.

The 'messy' inscriptions are in both Maori and English, the most explicit and striking of which fills the bottom half of the right-hand panel, and explicitly states '*TUHOE/ UREWERA/THEIR LAND*', below which are references to the Maori prophets Rua and Te Kooti, the warrior leader and founder of the Ringatu Church, and the subject of Maurice Shadbolt's excellent novel *Season of the Jew*. The left panel has a long inscription against the backdrop of a darkening sky. The centre panel contains a huge, creamy ochre tree, which stands like a sentinel, with the words 'TANE' ('God of the forest') and 'ATUA' ('God') at either side of the base, and there are further inscriptions in the green black hills that traverse the whole work.

On 5 June 1997 the Urewera mural was stolen from the Visitors' Centre. It happened in the middle of the night, quickly, a typical smash and grab, as if it had been a jar of sweets in a shop window. In the space of only two minutes the Centre was broken into and the alarm went off, the burglars entered the premises, set up a ladder and ripped the mural off the wall, raced back to their car and made their escape.

How can you take a picture off a wall so quickly and efficiently? In the case of the *Mona Lisa*, you had to have the professional know-how. But the McCahon mural was merely tacked to a board along the top edge, and easily enough removed from it. The method of its presentation might suggest some lack of professional competence and respect, but it was how McCahon designed the painting to be displayed. (In any case this was an improvement on an earlier period, in which the picture had been rolled up on top of a former Director's wardrobe, and exhibited in its place was … a map of New Zealand.)

How could anyone accomplish such a theft without inflicting significant damage? What could you do with the painting? Roll it up, or fold it, and stuff it into a car boot? Not likely to do it much good. But, according to Dame Jenny Gibbs, New Zealand's most important art collector and the holder of the finest McCahon collection in private hands, there was still reason to hope. 'McCahon', she explained, 'worked on heavy-duty canvas, and painted with normal house paints. The pictures are very resilient – I never hesitate to loan mine for exhibitions, whereas with artists who use less durable materials I am more circumspect.'

By the time the Park's area manager, Glenn Mitchell, got himself out of bed and hustled round to the Centre from his nearby cottage, the picture and thieves were gone. But there aren't many places to vanish to down at the lake. You can't speed on the unlit rustic byways, which New Zealanders call 'metal' roads, as they are made up of loose stone chippings. One phone call, five minutes after the theft, and both the Department of Conservation and the police were on their way to set up road-blocks. There could be no escape.

Only a damn fool could have hoped to get away with such a theft, unless they had a boat, a helicopter or at least some cunning plan to transfer the booty to an accomplice. The thieves had none of the above, but they got away with it anyway, because there is, from a burglar's point of view, no beating good old investigative incompetence. Forty-five minutes later – it was now two in the morning, so there wasn't much traffic – two Maori in a beaten-up van drew up to the road-blocks. The middle-aged driver, with a traditional Maori fully tattooed face ('moko'), pulled over as the van was waved to the side of the road. In the back a teenaged boy was sleeping on a mattress. Just off for a little spin, the driver explained, noting that his chum had had enough and nodded off. The Department of Conservation had no legal right to search the van, but the police did so in a cursory manner, before waving it through. The McCahon mural lay undetected under the mattress. It was not seen again for fifteen months.

It didn't take much time to find the (now burned-out) van and to identify the driver and his sleeping passenger. Within three weeks a reformed drug addict and dealer named Te Kaha and the seventeen-year-old Laurie Davis, who had a string of burglary charges pending, appeared in court. The police had them bang to rights, the only thing lacking being evidence. Nothing connected them to the burning of the van, to the Visitors' Centre or to the painting. The case foundered and was dropped.

The Te Urewera region is a sparsely populated portion of the central eastern North Island, largely inhabited by the Tuhoe, with scattered small, demoralised settlements, low educational standards and considerable economic depriva- tion. The most profitable local cash crop is marijuana, a good deal of which is smoked before it hits the wider markets. The local people may be united by familial and tribal fealty under the influence of the local meeting centres, known as Marae, but many are often broke and desperate. The area has become a breeding ground for Tuhoe activists, some of them patient and well organised, others of whom preach violent revolution to bands of stoned teenagers ready to contemplate a fight, only not just now. Local police, often accused of racism by the locals, keep an eye out, but not much tends to happen.

No ransom for the painting was demanded, no manifesto issued in the name of its new possessors. But if the thieves were curiously silent, the rest of the nation was resound- ingly horrified. The theft was front-page news for weeks. If the picture was gone, who had it? And, more impor- tantly from the point of view of its possible retrieval, why? Though suspicion had fallen upon Tuhoe activists, there was nothing conclusively to link any of them to the crime. Even Tame Iti, a local firebrand promoter of both himself and his many causes, was uncharacteristically silent on the issue, which only added to the general suspicion that he had something (a painting perhaps) to hide. Born on a railway train in 1952, Iti has been travelling and fellow-travelling, ever since. As a young man, he protested against apartheid and the Vietnam War, journeyed to China to take in the Cultural Revolution, admired the Black Panthers and joined the New Zealand Communist Party, before settling down – having picked up a few insurrectionary tips – to the cause of Tuhoe nationalism.

With his full facial moko, which he has described as 'the face of the future', and a penchant for exposing his buttocks in public as a form of insult, Iti has provoked and self-displayed like the performance artist he was eventually (if not for long) to become. He has run for Parliament three times, and once fired a shotgun at the national flag in order to make the Pakeha 'feel the heat and smoke' as the Tuhoe have for almost two hundred years.

You want suspects? You've got them. The increasingly frustrated Detective Inspector Graham Bell, head of the police investigating the theft – in the imaginatively named 'Operation Art' – concentrated his efforts on interrogating the locals. Most knew that Te Kaha had been involved, but no one was willing to say so. Everyone in the area was questioned repeatedly, reports on suspicious meetings and journeys were logged, phones were (by all accounts) tapped. Nothing came of it, except that the locals felt harassed, and feeling against the police, always inflammable, heated up dangerously. If they knew where the painting was hidden, they were less and less likely to say so, or even to wish to safeguard it.

More or less a year had now passed: if the Tuhoe had the picture, surely it was time for them to say so, to indicate where it was – if it still existed – and to make a demand of some sort? When the demand came, though, it was from a surprising source. In June 1998 a criminal lawyer named Christopher Harder, who had a well-earned reputation for seeking the limelight, contacted Jenny Gibbs, hoping to arrange a meeting with Tame Iti and Te Kaha to negotiate a return of the picture. Gibbs was a shrewdly chosen inter-mediary: regularly described as the most influential woman in New Zealand, she is a patron of the arts as well as an art collector, and has a number of talented and influential Maori friends, including the writer Witi Ihimaera and the painter Ralph Hotere, and a history of fighting for the arts. And – this was apparently crucial – she also had access to her (separated) husband's helicopter.

She was aware that a member of the staff of New Zealand's National Gallery, Te Papa in Wellington, had already made a secret visit to the Ureweras in the hope of negotiating the picture's return. But it was unclear what the two Maori actually wanted. Money was mentioned but never actively pursued, perhaps because this would have catapulted their actions from the political to the merely mercenary. What was perfectly clear, though, was that the thieves had never anticipated such a fuss, and had badly under-estimated the importance (and value) of the mural. They were now seeking a way to give it back, save face and stay out of jail.

The two Maori soon met Gibbs at her house (really a private art gallery) on Paritai Drive, which is one of

Auckland's prime locations, with views over Okahu Bay, where she lives with three devoted and disarmingly yappy small poodles, who suffer from the mass delusion that they are capable of protecting her and her treasures. Gibbs had insisted from the outset that, if there was any question of a ransom, she would not be party to any negotiations, but took immediately to her Maori visitors: 'I looked at their eyes and decided that they were people I could trust', she said. This testified (depending on who you asked) either to her considerable acuity or to breath-taking gullibility. It was going to be interesting to find out which.

Over the next few months Gibbs tried to establish that the thieves could trust her as well, and her new contacts soon dropped their association with the lawyer Christopher Harder. Te Kaha was often seen with Gibbs, both at her home and socially, and rumours of a relationship flourished. Neighbours complained about the pair of moko-ed visitors, a rare species on Paritai Drive, and presumably felt racially and socially unsafe. Gibbs was lampooned in the press, and parallels with Leonard Bernstein's hosting of the Black Panthers at a cocktail party (see Tom Wolfe's *Radical Chic*) were suggested. Obscene phone calls in the middle of the night sneered that she 'liked a bit of black cock'. Through it all Gibbs kept her head up and her goal clear: she was trying to get the McCahon back. That was all that really mattered.

Inspector Bell, however, regarded her as the foolish dupe of the two totally *un*trustworthy Maori activists, and suggested that she was significantly impeding his investigation. She wasn't, but she certainly wasn't helping him very much. She was pursuing her own agenda. Witi Ihimaera describes her as 'sturdy and indestructible. If you were on the *Titanic* with her, she'd organize everyone to hold hands and climb to the bow rail and she'd be telling you that everything was going to be fine.'

Which is high praise. But the *Titanic* sank, and things were not fine. Nor was it clear that McCahon's painting was likely to be recovered. Tame Iti and Te Kaha were under severe pressure from feisty local voices, demanding that the painting be burned, or snipped into pieces and sent in the post (it was never clear to whom). Once she was told that the painting was now buried, Gibbs gave the two Maori 'a very large roll of bubble wrap and a lot of tape' to make sure it was safely entombed, and was relieved when it was reported that the rewrapping had been successful.

It took Gibbs a few months, and a lot of apparently enjoyable social time, plus several visits to the Urewera region, before she was promised the safe return of the picture. There were a number of false starts: 'You couldn't call them reliable', Gibbs observed wryly about Te Kaha and Tame Iti, who had repeatedly assured her of their intention to return the painting. Finally Gibbs was informed that 'tonight's the night!' and driven in the back of her car, having promised to keep her eyes shut, to an unknown destination in Auckland. When she next opened her eyes, the painting was in the back. It was taken immediately to the Auckland Museum of Art, where the necessary restoration work could be done.

The damage was far more extensive than the optimistic Gibbs would have suspected. The picture had been torn from the wall, folded roughly before it was put under the mattress, then rolled up for burial. It was dirty, and so badly crushed, creased and abraded that paint was missing along the fold lines. On the edges of the canvas there was some stretching and distortion, which may ease somewhat as the painting is rehung. Though it was possible to ameliorate much of the damage and retouching was done with gouache, the new paint can certainly be seen under raking light.

Te Kaha pleaded guilty to the theft, claiming that it was, from the onset, politically motivated:

> McCahon was a taste of what it feels like to have some-thing taken from you against your will and be powerless to stop it. The plan was always to show what it feels like ... I can take you back into Urewera, I can take you back into Tuhoe and show you land and pa sites [defensive earthworks] that have been destroyed. I can even show you people that have been destroyed ... people that are wasted. But why destroy a painting? At the end of the day it would mean sinking to the level of the people who had done things to Tuhoe.

Hearing the case, Judge Thorburn accepted the argument in mitigation and sentenced Te Kaha to community service at the Auckland Museum of Art, while Laurie Davis was sent to jail. Unbowed, Te Kaha continued to protest about the historical injustice that took the Tuhoe lands from them, and predicted 'an IRA type situation' unless the Tuhoe lands were restored and nationhood granted. In 2006 a group of Tuhoe activists, led by Tame Iti, were arrested under the 2002 Terrorism Suppression Act for having established, or at least encouraged, a group of guerrilla-style 'training camps' deep in the Ureweras, where lessons were apparently given in rudimentary bomb-making, and a range of nasty firearms were in regular use. IRA manuals were found, and texts pledging to 'kill the white motherfuckers' were cited by the prosecution.

Following so closely upon the Al Qaeda attack on the World Trade Center in New York, the New Zealand legislation, and response to the Tuhoe activists, were out of proportion to the admittedly worrying nature of their activities. You don't have to agree with the lawyer for the defence that this was just a bunch of teenagers larking about inappropriately to see clearly that they were not terrorists. Though it took five years, during which the framing of the 2002 Act was described by no less a person than New Zealand's Solicitor-General as 'unnecessarily complex, incoherent and as a result almost impossible to apply to the domestic circumstances in this case', the Urewera Four, as Iti and his cohorts were known, were found not guilty of all the major charges against them.

They got away with a lot. A lot of provocation, a lot of big talking, a lot that – in other cultures – might well have led to jail sentences. The guerrilla training, like the theft of the painting earlier, was symbolic. The thieves didn't really intend to destroy it, any more than the inflamed teenagers intended mass murder. The McCahon mural was better lost than found: it had a more potent message, and would resonate longer in the collective memory if it stayed buried. Tacked to a wall, it was just another painting, however fine; lost, it became a potent symbol of the dispossession of an entire people.

We are familiar with the hostility that extreme left-wing movements and fanatical groups can have to art establishments. Marinetti, Apollinaire and Picasso bombastically demanding the burning of museums, but instead merely pilfering from them occasionally. A real fanatic is quick to burn, while your revolutionary rhetorician merely wishes to shock. Witness the destruction of the ancient carved Buddhas of Bamiyan in 2001 by the Afghan Taliban, or the systematic destruction of the artefacts of the past by the Red Guards or the Khmer Rouge: regimes under which the mere terms 'intellectual' and 'artist' were abusive, and could lead to the killing fields. Sweep away the old to prepare for the new! Create a future fresh and unencumbered! Down with art! But there is, still, a long way to go from Marinetti to Pol Pot.

But to the Tuhoe, to Te Kaha and Tame Iti, none of these arguments or instances was of any interest. Nor was the McCahon picture itself: though Jenny Gibbs tried to interest the two Maori in McCahon's work, she acknowledges that they never engaged with it. 'They didn't care about the painting,' she observes, 'it was never the point. It was just something the loss of which would be deeply felt and create a response that would highlight the cause of the Tuhoe, and the much larger losses that had been imposed upon them.'

We are accustomed in these liberal times to talking of the sanctity of human life, and would hesitate, for fear of the consequences, to talk of the sanctity of art. Sanctity refers to that which is of supreme importance. But let's put a hypothetical to ourselves: a child is kidnapped, and the ransom demanded is the Urewera mural, or even the *Mona Lisa*.

And don't tell me we cannot negotiate with kidnappers or hostage takers. That is exactly what we *must* do. What do they *want*? A night at the Ritz? A ticket to the Cup Final? No problem. A Picasso print? It's yours! The *Mona Lisa*?

No! Alas, let the child die. So: a painting can be more valu-able than a human life. How about two human lives? Or a hundred thousand? I have a bomb, and unless you give me Picasso's *Guernica*, I will blow up Basingstoke! Hmmm. Time to think ...

Tame Iti and Te Kaha remind us that paintings like the Urewera mural do not exist for 'art's sake' but have complex and often conflicting cultural meanings, and the weight that they carry depends on your point of view. After the painting had been returned, Jenny Gibbs said that she had 'learned a lot': it was, she observed, 'a very clever scheme. I obviously don't approve of stealing a painting ... but they have had so much stolen from them.' She recognised clearly that she had been dealing with serious people, and a serious issue. The theft of the Urewera mural (unlike the theft of the *Mona Lisa*, in which a stink of farce and veniality prevails) brings into question many of our cherished, and frequently unex-amined, notions about art and its relations to our lives, and the lives of others.

But aren't we admonished to respect art for art's sake? I've never understood what 'art' is, such that it should have a 'sake.' Persons do, though, and sometimes our attitudes to people and our respect for art collide in unexpected and unsettling ways. I suspect that Jenny Gibbs would have entirely understood, perhaps sympathised if only fleetingly, if the mural had been destroyed. If not – she is an art col-lector, after all – it is certainly a line of thought that would have occurred to Colin McCahon. His sense of the deep symbolic potential of place would have been shared by the Tuhoe, and might well have been incomprehensible to most contemporary Pakeha. As he said, in 1977: 'You bury your heart, and as it goes deeper into the land. You can only follow, it's a painful love, loving a land. It takes a long time.'

The Visitors' Centre is now closed, condemned 'because of leaks' (water gets in, paintings get out) and resulting wet rot. And McCahon's great Urewera mural, after a whistle-stop tour of a number of provincial galleries, now resides in the Auckland Gallery, where it is still undergoing restoration and in which it will eventually hang until a new Visitors' Centre at the lake is built. But neither the room nor the light nor the ambience at the Art Gallery will be quite right for McCahon's masterpiece. Hamish Keith, a distinguished art historian and former Director of the Arts Council of New Zealand, observed: 'I have no doubt at all that the work, if removed from the Park Headquarters at Urewera National Park, would find some safe home. Simply to remove the painting from the context for which it was conceived is, however, little short of an act of vandalism.'

It is unclear when some new Visitors' Centre will open to the public, but there can be no one who doesn't wish for the return of the mural to its natural habitat, for the enjoyment of all those who may come to see it, and because it is as inte-gral a part of that landscape, now, as Lake Waikaremoana itself. It is a great painting, even ignoring its history. As sym-pathetic as one is to the cause of the dispossessed Tuhoe tribe, one can only be grateful that they eventually returned the picture. Political causes and allegiances, like personal ones, come and go, and it is the purpose and nature of art both to reflect such differences and to transcend them. To stand as the last word, the greatest legacy mankind and its artists have provided to the transience of things, and to reside in permanent opposition to that which, finally but surely, passes. No justification, surely, can be adequately adduced for the destruction of an artistic masterpiece.

That's the common view, but I'm not sure Jenny Gibbs would have shared it wholeheartedly. Neither do I.

3

'Half-Witted': Graham Sutherland's Portrait of Winston Churchill

On the occasion of his eightieth birthday, on 30 November 1954, Winston Churchill was honoured by both Houses of Parliament. His speech in Westminster Hall was worthy of the occasion, as he looked back upon his career and achievements:

> I have never accepted what many people have kindly said – namely, that I inspired the nation. ... Their will was resolute and remorseless, and as it proved unconquerable. ... It was the nation and the race dwelling all round the globe that had the lion's heart. I had the luck to be called upon to give the roar.

But the old lion was tired, and acknowledged that his days of political life, after some fifty-four years, were almost over:

> I am now nearing the end of my journey. ... I hope I still have some service to render. However that may be, whatever may befall, I am sure I shall never forget the emotions of this day.

He resigned as Prime Minister less than a year later, but in the remaining ten years of his life still found the energy to write the six volumes of *A History of the English-Speaking Peoples*. He also produced a large number of competent, slightly old-fashioned (though with occasional Impressionist touches) oils on canvas, which gave him great satisfaction. Though he did some reasonably accomplished portraits, he preferred landscapes. 'Trees don't complain', he observed in wry acknowledgement of the fact that sitters for portraits frequently do.

The Parliamentary celebrations, in front of an audience of some 2,500 people, were broadcast live on BBC television. As the aged Prime Minister delivered his speech, both the live and televised audiences were faced not merely by the orator but also by the life-size portrait of him, commissioned to mark the occasion, which was hanging on the wall behind him. It was by Graham Sutherland, one of the celebrated artists of the day, whose paintings of bomb damage during the Blitz are amongst the most memorable artistic images of the Second World War.

The portrait of Churchill was arresting, and it would have been impossible for a member of the audience not to have cast his eye back and forth between the man himself and the image in oil behind him. The picture was by no means intended simply to flatter its subject. It had 'truth' as its aim, as serious portraiture must: a good portrait, gently or brutally, lays its subject bare. Churchill is seated, leaning – almost teetering – slightly to his right, facing outwards with an expression which is at once bewildered and irascible, stripped of the fund of loquacious good humour that was so characteristic of him in his prime. He retains a

Winston Churchill overshadowed by Graham Sutherland's sombre portrait, which he hated.

stoic authority, though, and the head has the monumental quality of a Roman bust. This is an old man, sadly aware of the decline of his powers, full of bitter regret, the predominant tones being rust and brown. Churchill's response to such colouration was distinctly sniffy: 'I cannot pretend to be impartial about the colours. I rejoice with the brilliant ones, and am genuinely sorry for the poor browns.'

The portrait ends at the sitter's ankles, as if he were, now, incapable of locomotion. Directly below the painting a bank of flowers was in place, as if offered at a funeral service. Studying this image, a viewer might well have acknowledged that the portrait was fair comment. When he had been elected in 1951, Churchill had concealed the fact that he had suffered a major stroke, and the intervening three years had only hastened his decline. On the day of the celebrations, he rose magnificently to the occasion, but it was one of the last of his great speeches. He was exhausted, and his health was declining rapidly, but he had not fully accepted that his time was over. The portrait – like that of Wilde's Dorian Gray – starkly revealed the truth. What we see, in the apt words of the *Guardian*'s art critic at the time, is 'a reactionary curmudgeon surrounded by the shades of night'.

Sutherland's portrait had been commissioned by the Prime Minister's Parliamentary colleagues as a birthday gift, to be retained by him during his lifetime, and afterwards hung at Westminster. Churchill and his wife were, of course, already familiar with the portrait, for the Prime Minister sat for it at Chartwell, his home in Kent, at various sessions between August and November of 1954. He was, apparently, a 'grumpy and difficult' subject, who tended to slump into his chair after a few drinks at lunch and was roused into good humour only by the presence of his dog. The process was eased by Lady Churchill's reaction to the artist, whom she called 'a most attractive man ... a Wow!' When she first saw the finished picture at Kenneth Clark's home, in October, she was immediately taken by its 'truthfulness', but after a time she began to feel that it cast her husband as 'a gross and cruel monster'. This was an ominous sign: Clementine clearly felt it not merely her right, but her duty, to monitor images of the great man, and had previously destroyed pictures of him by both Walter Sickert (in 1927) and Paul Maze (in 1944). Maze, ironically, had given Churchill some tips about how to paint.

Churchill saw the finished portrait some weeks later, and was chagrined by its 'malignant' quality, though he generously resolved to accept it in the spirit in which it was offered, announcing with studied ambiguity that 'the portrait is a remarkable example of modern art. It certainly combines force and candour.' Though he was not disposed airily to dismiss modernity ('Without tradition, art is a flock of sheep without a shepherd. Without innovation, it is a corpse'), he had little taste for it. His private response to the alleged 'truthfulness' of the portrait was that the posture and expression made him look as if he were straining on the toilet, and that 'it makes me look half-witted, which I ain't.'

So: if the Churchills so disliked the finished image, why hadn't they said so during the sittings, when they were presumably able to inspect the portrait as it developed? The answer is that Sutherland's finished product differed considerably from the studies done at Chartwell. For many of the sittings the Prime Minister was dressed in his Knight of the Garter robes (which do not appear in the final picture), and the surviving sketches, many of them now at the National Portrait Gallery, show him in a gentler, and more respectful, light. He would hardly have anticipated the gross truthfulness, if that is what it is, of the finished product. It must have been particularly galling, and humiliating, for the Prime Minister as he stood before the offending object, live on the BBC, to thank his colleagues for a gift which offended him so egregiously.

I don't know who was responsible for the choice of Graham Sutherland as Churchill's portraitist, but they – I presume some committee or other – made a bad mistake. It might have been because they knew too little about contemporary art, or too much. The result would have been the same: an ignorant selection panel would have chosen the most highly rated artist of the day, on the assumption that such a choice would signify the depth of affection in which Churchill was held. Similarly, a knowledgeable panel might have come to the same conclusion, only they would have reached it themselves. In either case they would have been wrong.

Though Graham Sutherland's work has fallen into disregard – since his death in 1980 there has been no English retrospective of his work – in 1951 he was at the height of his reputation, and powers. He shared the Venice Biennale exhibition of English art in 1952 with Edward Wadsworth, and had a retrospective at the Musée National in Paris in the same year. His reputation in Paris was, as Kenneth Clark remarked, higher than any English artist since Constable, which may simply show how little taste, or discrimination, the French have for English painting. But in England, too, he was regarded as the leading painter of his time. He was, claimed Douglas Cooper in his 1961 book on the artist, 'the most distinguished and the most original English artist of the mid-20th century ... no other English painter can compare with Sutherland in the subtlety of his vision, in the forcefulness of his imagery and in the sureness of his touch.'

Sutherland's own description of his artistic disposition is worth citing here. His twisted landscapes, bedecked with thorns (surely generated by his Roman Catholicism), render the apparent beauties of nature in a sinister light:

> the closeness of opposites in life has always fascinated me. That is to say the tension between opposites. The precarious balanced moment – the hair's breadth between – beauty and ugliness – happiness and unhappiness – light and shadow.

The description suggests an affinity with his contemporary Francis Bacon, in some ways an unlikely comparator but a friend of Sutherland's, and some say an influence. Or might it have gone the other way?

William Boyd, commenting on Sutherland's *Gorse on a Sea Wall* (1939) – 'twisted, tortured, organic form(s) set more or less centrally against bold opaque panels of colour' – sees clear evidence that Sutherland precedes Bacon in such agonised painting, and is an influence on his development. Bacon rejected the claim in typically camp manner, calling Sutherland 'such a petty pilferer ... She never had the nerve for grand larceny.' His pictures, he claimed, owed nothing to Sutherland, whose portraits he dismissed as nothing more than 'coloured snaps'. Indeed, remarks the art critic William Feaver, to a contemporary eye the Sutherlands merely look like 'Bacons gone wrong'.

Not that Sutherland was known as a portraitist. Indeed, what is often described as his 'first' portrait was painted as late as 1949, a £300 commission from Somerset Maugham. The finished painting hung in the writer's Villa Mauresque in Provence for a time, until Maugham could no longer stand the sight of it and hid it away. It shocked him, he said with some attempt at grace, that 'here was far more of me than I ever saw myself.' His friends, deeply offended on his behalf, simply loathed it. Max Beerbohm remarked that at least Maugham would no longer need to be caricatured, while the portrait painter Gerald Kelly remarked that it made him look like a madam in a Shanghai brothel. Yet, seen from a distance of many years, the picture has undeniable quality: set against a burned orange background, Maugham is perched on a cane chair, arms folded, his chin thrust imperiously into the air. His shoulders fall and slope alarmingly, as if he were melting, his scrawny throat cloaked in a scarlet scarf, elongated bony hand laid on the sleeve of a brown jacket, he looks remote and angry beyond any comprehension, including his own, befuddled by loss and age, and decrepitude. And, from what one knows of Maugham's later years, one might only say: fair enough.

The portrait was not merely representative but captured an inner reality, aimed itself at essence rather than appearance. In this sense the picture is not merely figurative but pre-figurative: an image of the senility, decay and rage that were still to come. This was Maugham as he would be in his dotage, and there was nothing likeable about it. Why should there be? It was, as the artist remarked a little tartly, *Art*. It is not the painter's business to flatter, but to render accurately the perceived truths of his sitter's nature. Sutherland makes the point explicitly:

> People today – superficially at least – are much more aware of what they think they look like and others look like: or what they think they look like or ought to look like. I think it is true that only those totally without physical vanity, educated in painting or with exceptionally good manners, can disguise their feelings of shock when confronted for the first time with a reasonably truthful image of themselves.

This bit of special pleading begs all the relevant questions – what *count*s as 'reasonably', as 'truthful', as an 'image of themselves'? Sutherland's major aversion is to the notion that a portrait should flatter, as if this were a form of toadying to the bloated self-image and self-importance of the sitter. No way. It was the aim of the artist – it was his *job* – to tell the *truth*. And the truth, by clear if curious implication, is rarely flattering. Lord Beaverbrook, presented by his colleagues with a specially commissioned Sutherland portrait of himself in 1954, could only remark: 'It's an outrage, but it's a masterpiece!'

None of Sutherland's portraits (others include Edward Sackville-West, Helena Rubinstein and Kenneth Clark) – with the notable exception of his handsome *self*-portrait of 1977 – makes his subject look attractive, or comfortable, much less admirable. They dissect, reduce and diminish. The sitters are viewed with a cold, reductive eye, generated by a relentless Christian vision that strips away pride to expose the frailty of the body with its appalling temptations and disgusting aspects, to test the spiritual reality beneath. All is vanity. Sutherland's pictures are almost as cruel as those of Francis Bacon and Lucian Freud – better painters to be sure, but both equally, if differently, distressed and fascinated by what it is to be a human being. There is nothing fond about them, nothing warm, little that honours the sitter's nature rather than the artist's vision.

Hence, I suppose, the Parliamentary panel may not have seen the portrait before it was too late, though reports of it might have reached them, had they asked around sufficiently. I presume they did not. What the selection panel did not do, palpably and culpably, was to consult, not the art world, but Churchill's own taste. Any visitor to Chartwell would have known that the Churchills had no disposition for the modern, as Winston's own pictures – both the ones he produced and the ones he owned – testified.

He had thought long, if not particularly deeply, about art. Painting for him was a 'pastime', a consuming hobby and source of delight. His pronouncements on the subject suggest the conspicuously satisfied amateurishness of his commitment:

> Leave to the masters of art trained by a lifetime of devotion the wonderful process of picture-building and picture creation. Go out into the sunlight and be happy with what you see.

He began painting after his unhappy departure from the Admiralty in 1915. Art as therapy? His account of that moment is revealing:

the change from the intense executive activities of each day's work at the Admiralty to the narrowly measured duties of a councillor left me gasping. Like a sea-beast fished up from the depths, or a diver too suddenly hoisted, my veins threatened to burst from the fall in pressure ... And then it was that the Muse of Painting came to my rescue – out of charity and out of chivalry, because after all she had nothing to do with me – and said, 'Are these toys any good to you? They amuse some people.'

He recalled this period in an essay of 1922, 'Painting as a Pastime', which was published in *The Strand*, and which was reprinted as part of his book of the same title (one of the most popular of his post-war works), which was published in 1948. In the same year he exhibited at the Summer Exhibition of the Royal Academy and was elected Honorary Academician Extraordinary, a title that seems slightly equivocal, as if to suggest that the recipient was not a *real* painter.

He was counselled against publishing the 1922 essay, for which he received £1,000, by his wife, Clementine, who worried that it would irritate professional painters and 'cause you to be discussed trivially' – that is, labelled an outright amateur. But, though Churchill valued Clemmie's advice and frequently followed it, that is what he *was*, and he made no pretence to the contrary: painting was 'great fun': 'I do not presume to explain how to paint, but only how to get enjoyment.'

He didn't get much enjoyment out of Sutherland's portrait. In due course, the festivities and celebrations over, the offending object was shipped to Chartwell, where it was conspicuous by its absence, Lady Churchill having vowed that it would 'never see the light of day'. Her husband, she said, had always disliked it and it had 'preyed on his mind'. It was destroyed at her request within a year or two of its presentation, though the family did not reveal the fact until after her death in 1977.

Sutherland described the action as 'an act of vandalism', though he acknowledged that 'I know Sir Winston didn't like it.' There followed a sustained, emotive and largely unfocused controversy in the media about whether Lady Churchill had, in fact, been right – or had the right – to destroy the portrait. Too little of the ensuing discussion made the salient point that the picture was a gift that was intended to revert to, and hang in, Westminster. The Churchills did not own it, and mere possession is certainly not nine-tenths of the law, otherwise every time you are lent something, or steal it, you could claim it as your own.

But let us assume that the Churchills did own the portrait, in which case there are several different points at issue, both moral and legal. Broadly framed, the most important question is this: do the rights of an owner of property override those of the public, which may benefit from something the owner has in his possession? You are allowed to destroy an important painting that you own, though it would clearly be wrong to do so. Yet with houses we are more demanding: if you have a house of historical significance, you cannot knock it down, or alter it significantly without consent. It belongs to you, to be sure, but it also belongs in some way to the nation. Should this not also be true of important works of art?

Perhaps the members of the Houses of Parliament might have claimed damages and costs from the Estate of

Clementine Churchill, but that would have been unseemly. More interestingly, Graham Sutherland (had he been French) could himself have pursued the matter, for English law (unlike French, which has a key concept of the *'right of integrity'* of the artist) does not protect artists from the destruction of their work. In any case, what did it matter? The portrait was gone, and no quantity of indignation or lawyers would bring it back.

No, to recover some simulacrum of the finished product there were only two possibilities. First, there were numbers of photographs of the picture, which at least preserved a record of it. Second, and more significantly, Sutherland did a number of quite finished preparatory works for the final portrait, which eventually found homes with collectors and galleries, including our own National Portrait Gallery. The most important of these studies, owned by Lord Beaverbrook, was exhibited at Canada House in 1999. It was regarded by many critics not merely as the finest portrait of Churchill ever painted, but as a masterpiece. But Churchill's grandson Winston (who was Beaverbrook's godson) nevertheless refused to be photographed next to the portrait. His grandfather, presumably, would have been offended.

And that, to me, is the point. The Sutherland portrait was commissioned as a gift on behalf of a grateful nation, in order to honour its recipient. It was a misjudgement by Sutherland, I believe, to produce such a grimly realistic portrait for such an occasion, but artists are like that. I think he should have refused the commission, given it the 'silent veto' that Churchill once employed when trying unsuccessfully to paint a pale blue sky.

Let me ask you this: if Winston Churchill, more than any

Englishman of the twentieth century, deserved our thanks and homage, was it not up to him – or to his wife – to decide if Sutherland's portrait was acceptable? Surely the purpose of the gift was not to offend its recipient. Suppose the Roman Senate had commissioned a bust of Caesar, to be presented to him when he returned from yet another triumphant tour subjugating the world. Let us suppose, too, that the sculptor had felt it incumbent to tell the truth, and produced a telling image of a bloated and ambitious tyrant, swollen with pride. Can you imagine the scene when the (offending) image was unveiled to the returned hero? Eyes would have rolled, and then heads. It would have been regarded by its recipient not as a mistake, or an example of artistic integrity, but as an unforgivable insult. And he would have been right.

I don't, of course, wish that a similar fate had befallen Graham Sutherland, but he is as culpable as my imagined artist. His commission, really, was to celebrate, not to tell the truth as he saw it. His painting may well have been a masterpiece, but I believe the Churchills had ample justification to destroy it, though I am sorry they chose to exercise it. (What they needed was a Jenny Gibbs to ferret it away, and ensure its restoration to Westminster.) When I said so, in a lecture at London's National Portrait Gallery, I invited the audience to vote on whether they agreed with me. The result? Ninety-seven votes that it was wrong of them to destroy the portrait, and one vote that it was justifiable. It's a landslide!

Presumably, then, I'm wrong? Life is short, and art is long? I presume that is what informed my audience's perception. If Churchill objected to how he looked in the portrait, in 200 years' time he *will* look like that, and too bad? The general position is fair enough, and my audience were probably right. But this was *Churchill,* and it was painted to honour him, and it didn't. To me that makes all the difference.

Anyway, you may have located something heated, indeed personal, in my dislike of most of Graham Sutherland's work, which is not caused entirely by the disrespect that he paid to Sir Winston Churchill. When I was a lecturer at the University of Warwick, one of the obvious ports of call for visitors, friends and relatives was the new Coventry Cathedral, not itself an exceptional building but movingly placed alongside the ruins of the old cathedral, and given a kind of gravitas through the conjunction. The new cathedral boasts an enormous (24m × 12m) Sutherland tapestry above the altar, *Christ in Glory,* which I was shocked by on first exposure, and came on repeated visits to dislike intensely. It is an absurd portrait, confused and bilious, the figure of Jesus in an anatomically strained position that could be either sitting or standing, but not quite stooping, clothed in an extraordinary garment that looks like a nappy that has morphed into some sort of robe, the lower half of this obscure garment shaped oddly like a beetle's shell.

The overblown grandiosity of the tapestry may arise because it is based on working drawings by the artist, which were then greatly enlarged by the weavers. What might work on a small scale becomes bloated and obvious on a large one: a slight line turns into a rope, a tiny subtle area of shading into a large blob. Any subtlety is thus lost, and the tapestry achieves its limited power merely because it is so big. On first seeing it, out of respect to both subject and artist, I tried desperately to withhold both judgement and sniggering, and tried to work out just what Sutherland could have intended. Some sort of 'truth' presumably. Certainly the size and placement of the tapestry give it an undoubted power. But whatever Sutherland's aim, the image is a pompous failure, an offence to the eye that diminishes what little aesthetic power the new cathedral itself may possess.

If this is Christ in Glory, I'd hate to see him on a bad day. If the burghers of Coventry had had any sense, they should have sent it back.

And the same goes for the Churchills.

4

A Ghost Story: James Joyce's
Et Tu, Healy

It's only a fragment, and it is impossible to make any serious claim for its quality. All that is known of the poem – no printed copy exists – are the following lines, with which it presumably closes:

> His quaint-perched aerie on the crags of Time
> Where the rude din of this century
> Can trouble him no more.

These shards carry a special power for me, as if I first heard them in the nursery. I seem, alas, to have set them on an internal loop to the tune of 'De Camptown Races', that catchy chronicle of running and gambling. It drives me crazy when I can't make it stop:

> Can trouble him no more! Trouble him no more!
> His quaint perched aerie on the crags of time
> Can trouble him no more!
> (Repeat)

Though the lines were produced by a nine-year-old, no one reading them at the time would have posited exceptional talent, for kids could write like this in the nineteenth century, if they were bright and had the right schooling. Oscar Wilde turned out reams of such stuff, and not only when he was a schoolboy.

I am over-stimulated by such juvenilia, like a bibliographic Lewis Carroll taking snapshots of little persons revealing themselves inappropriately. Is there something creepy about this literary priapism? I am a dealer in rare books, after all, and the blank spaces of this poem are an obsession of mine. I would rather read the unknown rest of it than fill in the gaps of my reading of any major poet, or discover an exciting new one. I am longing to know what opening it might have had, how it developed, and most of all what it looked like.

But what I really want is to own it, this cheaply printed broadside. I'm haunted by its absence, by the faint possibility of its discovery, by the unfinished business of that unpromising text. It is embarrassing, this greed, without scholarly or aesthetic dimension. *To be the only person who owns a copy.* To show it off, appear in the papers and on telly clutching it, reading its immature lines with as straight a face as possible. Howard Carter, returned from the young king's tomb, bearing lost treasure.

In the opening chapter of *A Portrait of the Artist as a Young Man* we overhear a violent family altercation over Christmas dinner, and though the book is a novel I have little doubt that such an event actually took place. Much of *A Portrait* is autobiographical, and many of the names, places and incidents were taken directly from the young Joyce's life. Parnell

James Joyce, aged six, dressed up as a sailor boy. Three years later he would rebrand himself as a poet.

had died only a couple of months earlier, and Joyce's father ('Simon') was in a rage about the circumstances of his death:

> – Really, Simon, you should not speak that way before Stephen. It's not right.
> – O, he'll remember all this when he grows up, said Dante hotly – the language he heard against God and religion and priests in his own home.
> – Let him remember too, cried Mr Casey to her from across the table, the language with which the priests and the priests' pawns broke Parnell's heart and hounded him into his grave. Let him remember that too when he grows up.
> – Sons of bitches! cried Mr Dedalus. When he was down they turned on him to betray him and rend him like rats in a sewer. Low-lived dogs! And they look it! By Christ, they look it!
> – They behaved rightly, cried Dante. They obeyed their bishops and their priests. Honour to them!
> – Well, it is perfectly dreadful to say that not even for one day in the year, said Mrs Dedalus, can we be free from these dreadful disputes!

In the following chapter, away at school at Clongowes, Stephen recalls the incident, and its effect on him:

> He saw himself sitting at his table in Bray the morning after the discussion at the Christmas dinner table, trying to write a poem about Parnell on the back of one of his father's second moiety notices. But his brain had then refused to grapple with the theme and, desisting, he had

covered the page with the names and addresses of certain of his classmates.

That seems right, the child's brain refusing to 'grapple' with what is, after all, his father's passion, not his own. Stephen's first poem in *A Portrait* is written years later, in early adolescence, and the haunting villanelle 'Are You Not Weary of Ardent Ways' has nothing of the second-hand about it. It describes the 'rude din' of adolescent desire, not of 'this century', and there are no metaphorical Eagles quaint-perched in their aeries on the crags of Time.

But it was the nine-year-old Joyce who, in 1891, composed the eulogistic verses that his younger brother Stanislaus later referred to as 'the Parnell poem'. (Joyce later sanctioned the Latinate title of '*Et Tu, Healy*'.) Stanislaus, to whose imperfect memory we owe the three lines with which I began, described the poem as 'a diatribe against the supposed traitor, Tim Healey, who had ratted at the bidding of the Catholic bishops and become a virulent enemy of Parnell, and so the piece was an echo of those political rancours that formed the theme of my father's nightly, half-drunken rantings'.

Stanislaus reports that John Joyce, delighted by his son's production, 'had it printed, and distributed the broadsheets to admirers. I have a distinct recollection of my father's bringing home a roll of thirty or forty of them.' He also remembered that, in the (largely destroyed) thousand-page first draft of *A Portrait*, later published under the title *Stephen Hero*, 'my brother referred to the remaining broadsheets, of which the young Stephen Dedalus had been so proud, lying on the floor torn and muddied by the boots of the furniture removers' when the family moved from Blackrock in 1892.

Stannie's memory was confirmed by John Joyce himself, who when asked whether the broadsheet really existed by the bookseller Jake Schwartz, of the Ulysses Bookshop in Holborn, responded: 'Remember it? Why shouldn't I remember it? Didn't I pay for the printing of it and didn't I send a copy to the Pope?' But repeated inquiries to the Vatican Library by bibliographic busybodies since that time have not unearthed this copy of the poem. Presumably it was thrown out – can they really preserve every insignificant titbit, much less one in praise of an adulterer and sinner, that is sent in for the Pope's approval? – but it's a beguiling thought that it might still be there, in some drawer or other.

When you are in search of treasure – surely the animating archetype of collecting and dealing – you have to search the caves, to hunt for the rare and desirable. I began collecting as a boy, laid down a lifetime pattern of wanting and hunting, of desire, frustration and occasional satisfaction. When I was seven, in 1951, Topps (a company previously best known for making Bazooka bubblegum) began issuing baseball cards, and I, like all of my friends, was immediately obsessed by them. For a nickel you got five cards and a flat piece of gum that was unchewably stiff, nastily over-sugared and invariably thrown away. The ideal was to own all of the twenty-five players on your team – mine was the Washington Senators, though I switched allegiance to the Brooklyn Dodgers when we moved to Long Island in 1954. Topps knew how to get you hooked: most of the cards were common, but the most desirable ones were issued in much smaller quantities. We boys would buy and buy, yearning to fill our gaps. At Topps there must have been an avalanche of nickels rolling in.

I needed the Senators' first baseman, Mickey Vernon, my favourite player, who led the American League in batting in 1953. His card was scarce. I bought and bought, leafed avidly through the five cards: wrong teams! Wrong players! No Mickey. I offered remarkable enticements to a friend who had one, and who taunted me with it. Knowing how much I yearned for my hero – in owning the card you magically incorporated the person – he declined, reckoning he'd get a better deal in the future. I cajoled, pleaded, ranted. No dice. I could visit Mickey but not acquire him. (At six, I wrote my first short story, a scrappy couple of sentences in crayon, which must have taken all of fifteen minutes to compose. It was called *A Friend for Mickey*. I was unaware of the relationship to my later compulsion.)

To outflank my mean friend, whom I was soon to drop, I went to a shop, where the choices were as wide as the prices were intimidating. The only dealer I knew sold used comics and baseball cards in tiny premises on Long Island. I remember a podgy, red-faced old man (most men were old) in a soiled Yankees shirt, with lank grey hair and a bored expression. I don't remember if he had acne, but memory requires it, so I have given him some in deference to that archetypal nerd in *The Simpsons*, Comic Book Guy. On those interminable hot summer days Dad would drive me to the shop and watch benignly as I prowled about in the stifling gloom. Dust mites floated in the air, making me feel that I was under water like my fairground goldfish (Mickey), as I peered into glass cases at the rarities, or flicked through the commoner cards in the hope of finding one I needed.

Dad didn't collect anything himself – he had a large number of books, but they were casually put together rather than compulsively assembled – but he was amused by my ardour, and when we got back to my grandparents' bungalow, where we spent the summers, he would spend a few minutes with me as I installed my acquisitions in my collection. I shocked Granny Pearl by spending five dollars on a rare card that I'd been wanting for ages. I kept it on my bedside table for a week, and showed it off to envious friends, before putting it in the White Owl cigar box that Poppa Norman had given me, and forgetting about it. I'd been offered one or two tempting trades, but declined to part with my treasure except in a straight swap for a Mickey, which would have been fair. No deal. I regularly and intemperately accused Topps of unfair practices, which was right: manipulation of the market meant manipulation of me. Make something virtually unobtainable and any real collector will immediately yearn for it. Scarcity engenders need. Hunger is like that.

Collecting of this childish sort fades, in most boys, after adolescence. My stamp collections and Lionel trains went onto my closet shelf, from which they eventually, mysteriously, disappeared; my Topps cards in their cigar box, too, simply went away. I never regretted the loss of the stamps and trains, but the 1952 Topps became highly collectable in later years, and I must have had some valuable ones. (I don't remember if I had a 1952 Mickey Mantle rookie card, but they are worth up to $150,000 today.) And that, of course, is why they are valuable, as boy collector after boy collector shelved them, and myriad Moms threw them out in a clearup as the erstwhile fanatic went to college and entered that collecting latency period from which few emerged. Collecting is one of those boyish things that get put aside. There's something nerdy, something Comic Book Guy-ish, about an adult playing with train sets, picking up stamps with twee-zers, searching still for a Mickey Vernon. No, if you return to collecting as an adult, it is more often art, or furniture, rugs or ceramics perhaps. Or books, though not many go that route. There are not many book collectors, and almost no one understands them.

I don't know how I turned into a rare book dealer. It snuck up on me. My unappetising acquaintance the baseball card dealer hardly served as a role model – no one entering that dusty room could have thought, 'I want to be like him, that's just the job for me!'

You couldn't, in those days, train as a book dealer, and though there are now MA courses in the subject, I can't imagine they are worth doing. You learn the trade willy-nilly, by trial and (mostly) error. Because you pay for your mistakes, buying the wrong thing, or the right one at the wrong price, you learn quickly. During my time writing my D.Phil. at Oxford, I haunted the local used bookshops, and it became a kind of challenge for me to see if I could pay for my holidays by scouting – also called being 'a runner' (as in 'De Camptown Races', 'gwine to run all night, gwine to run all day') – and selling my purchases at a profit to members of the book trade. I had never heard, then, of *Et Tu, Healy*, or I would have looked.

It is a confirmation of both the obscurity and the intrinsic uninterestingness of *Et Tu, Healy* that there has been virtu-ally nothing written about it. No sustained consideration, no single article, just a few passing mentions, most of them decades ago. There's just not enough material to work on, even in the Joyce industry, where thousands of articles have been published about (almost) every possible topic. In my years as a university lecturer, when I occasionally taught courses on Joyce, I had no interest in *Et Tu, Healy*, lost or found. What did it matter? But I once contemplated writing a bibliomystery, as they are called, about a Russian diplomat and bibliophile who is being blackmailed because he is gay, and in order to raise the money composes a forgery of *Et Tu, Healy*, which he offers to the University of Texas for a million dollars. I never got further than that, though I liked my prospective title of *Et Tu, Borys* better than my half-imagined plot.

Et Tu, Healy is not a ghost (a book the publication of which has been announced, but never produced) in the strict bibliographic sense, but it's close enough for me. I encountered a real one as William Golding's bibliographer – a project that neither he nor I much enjoyed – when I discovered that there should have been an American printing of his first book (*Poems*, published in England by Macmillan in 1934), though no copies have been located. But there is something ambiguous about bibliographic ghosts. How can you tell, quite, if a book has been announced and never printed, or announced, printed and then lost?

Joyce's bibliographers, John Slocum and Herbert Cahoon, list *Et Tu* as item 1A: the very first of Joyce's books and pamphlets. (Indeed of Joyce's first four 'A' items, three are broadsides, including *The Holy Office* (1904) and *Gas From a Burner* (1912).) Given that Slocum and Cahoon is the first point of call for bibliographic queries about Joyce, it is disappointing how wrong they are about *Et Tu, Healy*, of which they cite seven lines, the three with which I began, plus the following four:

My cot, alas that dear old shady home
Where oft in youthful sport I played,
Upon the verdant grassy fields all day
Or lingered for a moment in thy bosom shade.

The authority for this attribution would appear to be Stanislaus's *Recollections of James Joyce*, but reference to that text makes it clear that Stannie is *distinguishing* these unprepossessing lines from those of the Parnell poem, not including them in it. In a letter to Harriet Shaw Weaver in November 1930, Joyce himself cites the quatrain, which he says he is going to use in *Finnegans Wake* in a game of Angels and Devil (here represented by Shawn), 'who maunders off into sentimental poetry of what I actually wrote at the age of nine'. There is something touchingly appropriate in the clumsiness of the phrase, from which a word or two seem to have been omitted. The game, and the poem, Joyce tells Miss Weaver, are soon 'interrupted by a violent pang of toothache after which he throws a fit', which may represent an act of literary self-criticism.

No, the Parnell poem is different from, and better than, 'My Cot Alas', even if they were written at much the same time. I do not think Joyce's category 'sentimental poetry' would have included *Et Tu, Healy,* which is written in an altogether different register. So we must reduce what we know of that text by more than half: our ghost is getting ghostlier.

There is usually a lag between an author's death and the arrival on the market of significant letters, inscribed books and manuscripts. The mother lode – material held by the author himself, his closest friends and family – often takes decades to emerge, having been passed down the generations until someone decides that the choice between some old letters or manuscripts and a manse in Provence is a no-brainer. Recent sales of such Joyce material have realised prices sufficient to throw in a modest yacht as well.

After three decades during which almost no significant Joyce manuscript material emerged, all of a sudden there has been such a quantity of it – letters, inscribed books, working notebooks, whole chapters of *Ulysses*, draft material for *Finnegans Wake* – that a newcomer might have supposed such sales were common, or that an assiduous forger had secreted himself in a Martello tower to produce it. Between 2004 and 2010 the National Library of Ireland, which previously lacked any significant Joyce manuscripts, spent over 10 million Euros on manuscript material for both *Ulysses* and *Finnegans Wake*. Descendants of Stanislaus Joyce, John Quinn (the New York lawyer and collector who purchased a manuscript version of *Ulysses* from Joyce in the 1920s) and Joyce's friend and amanuensis Paul Leon have all sold material that alters our understanding of Joyce's achievement. In addition, manuscripts emerging from a Paris bookseller have thrown new light on the history of the composition of both *Ulysses* and *Finnegans Wake*. And I am told that T. S. Eliot's library – which has been visited by only a handful of scholars – contains fourteen previously unrecorded letters from Joyce to Eliot.

The more material that is discovered, the more that is likely to emerge. There is a magnetic pull when new discoveries are announced and rewarded: it makes people search their attics that little bit more thoroughly, and reconsider whether now might just be the right time to sell. Might the recent glut of Joyce material, and its attendant publicity, not unearth that elusive copy of *Et Tu, Healy*? What if it showed up in some disregarded bureau, or interleaved in some old atlas or Dublin directory? Surely if there is one – surely there *is* one – it must be in Dublin somewhere.

In my world, when you're talking ghosts you're talking money. By now you'll be wanting to know how much a copy, if found, would be worth. My business is based on trading in unique material, and I should be able to figure this one out. What of previously lost pieces which have been found? In 2006 Bernard Quaritch Booksellers offered for sale the only known copy of Shelley's anonymous pamphlet the *Poetical Essay on the Existing State of Things*, previously assumed to be a ghost. Oddly enough, it too was written in support of a beleaguered Irish figure, a journalist called Peter Finnerty, who had been imprisoned for libel for denouncing the Foreign Secretary, Lord Castlereagh, for abusing Irish prisoners.

The price? Quaritch were asking a million dollars, the archetypal roundness of which suggests that they were arbitrarily assigning a value – like my forger Borys – not attempting accurately to calculate one. If it had been priced at $875,000, it would give one more confidence, carry an authority and suggest some specific computation, however spurious. What about other obscure pieces of juvenilia? There is Evelyn Waugh's *The World to Come: A Poem in Three Cantos*, printed when he was thirteen (£50,000?), and Edith Wharton's *Verses*, published when she was sixteen ($150,000?), but both are known in a few copies, and neither author compares to Joyce in market terms. Perhaps the comparison should be with other Joyce works? A nice example of the hundred signed copies of the first edition of

Ulysses is now worth £250,000. Majestic in its Aegean blue, this is the most desirable issue of the most important book of the century. Is *Et Tu, Healy* worth more than that? It isn't as beautiful, or as important, but it's rarer. It's a ghost.

Who'd buy it? I can think of a couple of private collectors, The National Library of Ireland would surely be interested, the University of Texas might stump up, and sometimes buyers emerge at auctions, mysteriously, and then retreat grasping their treasure into the obscurity from which they had momentarily emerged. At the Sotheby's auction of material from Stanislaus Joyce's family, someone – not one of the usual Joyce collectors – paid £240,800 for one of the erotic letters that Joyce wrote to his wife, Nora ('my wild-eyed whore'), in1909, pining with desire during a brief separation. Nobody knew who the buyer was, though rumours suggested Michael Flatley, the *Riverdance* hoofer, who is known to be building a library. Would he – if it is he – find an *Et Tu, Healy* even more exciting than his erotic letter?

But until confronted with a copy, he couldn't really say. No one could, not exactly. Books, like pictures, are valued by both hand and eye: they need to have some kind of visceral appeal, some crackle and pop, which Jeanette Winterson nicely calls the 'psychometry of books'. Perhaps the mystique might evaporate when an actual copy emerges and is seen for the trifle that it really is?

Let me ask around: if a copy came up at auction, how much do you predict it would fetch? (Though even this doesn't necessarily determine how much it is worth, because many items bought at auction are resold quickly and at a profit.) What would Tom Staley make of it? He is Director of the Harry Ransom Center at the University of Texas,

Austin, the greatest repository of modern literary material in the world, and himself a Joycean. His opinion would partly determine what a copy fetched, even if he wasn't the buyer.

Asked the question, he is curiously decisive: 'a million four', he predicts (in dollars).

'Would you be a buyer?'

He looks up, twinkling, instantly on the prowl.

'Have you got one?'

I'm flattered that he thinks I might, and sorry to disappoint both of us.

'I'd have to find a donor,' he says, 'but I could.'

Peter Selley, of Sotheby's Book Department in London, who has handled some sensational Joyce manuscript material and letters in the last few years, is less easy about predicting a value. Auctioneers are like that. The comparators, he feels, are the erotic letter and perhaps a spectacular inscribed *Ulysses*. An estimate of £300,000 to £500,000 perhaps? 'Though in an immediate sense it is a far less sexy item than the erotic letter, it does have the obvious huge draw of being absent from every major collection private and public, plus also tapping into the profound on-going interest here and in the US in Irish Nationalism.' Which is to say, who the hell knows?

There would be a fuss, as the proud owner – me? me! – showed off his treasure, though by a nice irony the text might not be allowed to be printed in its entirety, due to the assiduous protectiveness of the Joyce estate. The old eagle in his eyrie overlooking the world is not, in this instance, the ghost of the late Parnell but Stephen Joyce, the author's grandson and protector of all things Joycean. So litigious is he that even Christie's, when they illustrate a Joyce manuscript, have decided to blur the image discreetly, as if it were a model's pubic hair in an old-fashioned nudie picture. And though Joyce's previously published work is now out of copyright, it is unclear whether a newly discovered piece would be, or not. After all, it had been published – hadn't it? – so copyright should have lapsed. Can you copyright a ghost?

Never mind. Word would get out – *Gekoski has a copy!* – and I would have assuaged my interest, filled in the gaps and banished my ghost. The net effect of which, ironically, would be to diminish the interest of the poem, as one could see it finally for what it is, strip it of its black tulip numinosity. Bookselling fetishises objects, but usually they are more or less worth the fuss. In my office I once had – lucky me, all at the same time – Jacob Epstein's green bronze bust of T. S. Eliot, one of six copies produced in 1951; a copy of Dylan Thomas's first book, *18 Poems,* inscribed to his wife 'Dylan to Caitlin – lovingly, in spite' the inscription stained with beer, or tears, perhaps both; D. H. Lawrence's own copy of *The Rainbow*; a letter from Ezra Pound to T. E. Lawrence gossiping about Yeats and Conrad, and a pencil self-portrait done by Sylvia Plath at seventeen. (They're all gone now.) I am still moved by such material: it's stuff like this that keeps me going, makes the treasure-hunting worth the aggravation and frequent disappointments. These are objects worth making a fuss about.

But *Et Tu, Healy*? Fetishisation: 100, Object: 0. This fact, for surely it is that, locates something that lurks disturbingly at the heart of my form of life. There is something dangerous in unrestrained treasure-hunting, a lurking sense of futility, which I, on its occasional outbreaks, find incapacitating. All those expensive first editions, many with prices dependent on whether they still had their dust wrappers and what condition they were in, isn't there something ridiculous about this? Book collectors frequently remark that there is no sense in showing their collections to their friends – they just don't get it. A copy of the first edition of *Brighton Rock* in a dust wrapper? Yeah, whatever … It's not until they are told it's worth £50,000 – largely for the wrapper – that they pay attention, but mostly to the collector's pathology rather than to the over-valued object: 'What're you, crazy?'

At least they would have heard of *Brighton Rock*, might even have read it. What happens when you show them the tatty, recently discovered piece of million-dollar paper that is *Et Tu, Healy*? What would they say then? What would I?

Ambrose Bierce's *Devil's Dictionary* defines a ghost as the outward manifestation of an inner fear. This is fair enough: we are frightened of death, and those spooks in sheets are the objective correlative of our terror. As they hover in the night, hoo-ing and woo-ing, we are reminded of the evanescence of human life, its short span, the long emptiness to come. *Et Tu, Healy* plays a similar role in my life and is similarly charged: the rattling of its baby chains causes a frisson of anxiety in me, as if my book-dealing life had been dedicated to futile pursuits and meaningless goals. Has there been something unworthy about it, snuffling about like a pig for trifles?

Perhaps if *Et Tu, Healy* rejoined the world, I might look it in the eye, make an adjustment in our long relations and rid myself of my obsession. I wonder what it would look like? What title might it bear? Who would be named as the author? My bet is on Jas. A. Joyce, the name under which, some ten years later, he published his first few articles. James Joyce sounds a little, well, old for a nine-year-old. And surely not Jim Joyce, though that is how he was known in the family.

And what would we be left with? Just a rare piece of paper, a poem written by a little boy and published by a proud father, transformed too quickly from a touching memento to a scrap under the removal men's boots. A lovely thing in its way, with its loss built into its very nature, and once found, thoroughly forgettable. Just the only known copy of *Et Tu, Healy*, nothing haunting about that.

Perhaps then that quaint perched eyrie on the crags of time will trouble me no more. And if that happens, I will, perversely, rather regret it. Being haunted by a lost scrap and occasionally tormented by a repetitive inner tune is small enough price to pay for the delight of the chase, however futile it occasionally feels. That excitement is strong enough to resist its shadow, and the continued absence of *Et Tu, Healy* animates and amuses me, when it isn't a source of depression.

I hope it never gets found. I prefer it lost.

Unless, of course, it's me who finds it.

5

Do It Yourself: The *Oath of a Freeman*

Though I can accept the absence *Et Tu, Healy* with a degree of equanimity, I am still tempted to go out and hunt for one. The world of dealing and collecting, of museums and curators, of connoisseurship and scholarship, rests on an underlying and animating archetype. Many essential human activities are like that. For schoolteachers, it is passing on the wisdom of the tribe to the young; for lawyers, ensuring that justice and representation are widely available; for doctors, that all are entitled to healthcare. And for a serious dealer or collector? That the treasure hunt must go on: there are buried, unlocated, misunderstood, misrepresented objects of every kind which are of value both commercial and cultural, and are essential to our understanding of ourselves. It is our job to find, to understand, and to preserve them.

Where to look for an *Et Tu*? I might, after all, apply to the Vatican Library and do whatever they would allow in the way of poking about. They have, after all, recently opened their enormous archives to the public. Maybe it's in there? Or I might wangle myself onto the news and TV in Ireland by offering a substantial reward for anyone who could locate a copy. A million dollars might concentrate a lot of minds.

There is one further possibility, of course. I might make

one myself. Though I once contemplated writing my *Et Tu, Borys* thriller, I never got far enough in my wayward imaginings to work out how such a forgery might be produced. But how difficult can it be? (There is the nice precedent of a similar fantasy in Doris Langley Moore's 1959 novel *My Caravaggio Style*, in which a forged copy of Byron's *Memoirs* enters the market.) So all I would need to do is to find a competent and impecunious Irish poet – plenty of those about – and get him to compose some childish pastiche on the death of Parnell. Obtain some paper stock – simply remove a blank page or two out of a book published around 1890 – and make sure the ink and typefaces are contemporary with it. After printing, let the finished article sit in the bright sunlight for a few hours to age a bit. Rub a bit of dust onto it. Fake up some sort of provenance (found between the covers of an old Dublin almanac!) Hey presto: a million dollars plus, with a following wind and a sufficiently enthusiastic buyer.

There can be no one in the rare book and manuscript world – dealer, collector, curator or auctioneer – who has not occasionally pursued a similarly criminal line of thought, though (of course) in fantasy we always assume someone else is doing the forging and gorging, and secretly rather admire them. The nerve, the resources, the vision! In an environment in which the quiet pursuit of scholarship dominates, and commerce is conducted with discreet gentility, it is nice to imagine a little covert mayhem. We're always too nice to each other, rare book people. There is very little by way of blackmail, and though we can envy each other to the point of vice, we are rarely homicidal.

There is, after all, the case of Mark Hofmann. Reasonably

Would you buy a used manuscript from this man? The forger and murderer Mark Hofmann.

well known as a dealer and sometime collector in the rare book and manuscript world in the early 1980s, Hofmann was universally regarded as a queer fish, later described in the *New York Times* as a 'scholarly country bumpkin'. Self-effacing, and with a creepy limp handshake, he was nevertheless more than tolerated in the rare book trade. He was quite active at the major book fairs, and had a knack of 'regularly producing' (as one rare book dealer put it) just what people wanted. He seemed to have both a good eye and good sources of material, and such dealers always do pretty well, however unprepossessing their characters. Maybe, in fact, such an ineffectual persona is a positive advantage, in that it makes your fellows and customers confident that they are not in the company of a shark. Surely such a Caspar Milquetoast (a 1920s' American cartoon character described by his creator as 'the man who speaks softly and gets hit with a big stick') was both harmless and trustworthy?

Neither of the above. (I've always suspected that Caspar Milquetoast would have made a good serial killer.) And Mark Hofmann had plenty to hide. He has been described as 'the most skilled forger this country has ever seen' by the manuscript dealer and expert on forgery Charles Hamilton, who added ruefully, 'He fooled me – he fooled everybody.' This must have been extra-pleasing to Hofmann, for Hamilton's book *Great Forgers and Famous Fakes* was one of his most valued reference books. Presumably he learned a lot from it.

He was in a distinguished tradition, and at the top of his trade. The only other possible contender for the Oscar for Best Forger would be T. J. Wise, the eminent bibliographer and scholar of the late Victorian world, who was only unmasked as an assiduous forger after his death, so eminent was he, and so anxious were his accusers that his old age be unperturbed by scandal. The neutrally titled *An Enquiry into the Nature of Certain Nineteenth Century Pamphlets*, by John Carter and Graham Pollard, was therefore only released (in 1934) after Wise's death. It established beyond doubt that the old scholar was a fraud and a criminal. But Wise, though undoubtedly a biblio-scoundrel of the highest order – forger of pamphlets ostensibly by great English poets (including Matthew Arnold, Elizabeth Barrett Browning, George Eliot, Meredith, Ruskin, Shelley, Tennyson and Thackeray), some of the pamphlets wholly 'new,' others with false dating – was a rank amateur compared to Hofmann, limited in range and ambition. He may have razored out pages of Shakespeare's First Folio from the copies at the British Library, in order to complete copies that he later sold, but, all in all, he was a petty criminal.

Hofmann, in his more ambitious way, was something of a genius, the kind of worthy antagonist Sherlock Holmes would have been glad to unmask: *The Case of the Murderous Forger*. Born in 1954 (on the anniversary of Pearl Harbor), the young Hofmann was the son of devout Mormons, an Eagle Scout, and by all accounts, a curious and active child, interested in chemistry and magic, as well as collecting stamps and coins. His description of his early years is fascinating:

As far back as I can remember I have liked to impress people through my deceptions. In fact some of my earliest memories are of doing magic and tricks. Fooling people gave me a sense of power and superiority ... When I was about 12 years old I began collecting coins. Soon afterwards I figured out some crude ways to fool other collectors by altering coins to make them appear more desirable. By the time I was 14 I had developed a forgery technique which I felt was undetectable.

When you add to these precocious interests and abilities the fact that he also enjoyed bomb-making with his friends, setting off the occasional explosion in the safety of the desert, all of the skills and indicators were in place for an interesting future. In 1973 he began a term of duty for the Mormon Church knocking on doors in search of English converts, though he later claimed he had lost his faith some years earlier and had only gone to England because it had been expected of him. From his base in Bristol, Hofmann began exploring the local bookshops, collecting material relating to the Mormons, schooling himself in the major antiquarian texts and their authors.

If you are going to become a forger, start with what you know. After a brief and unpromising period as a medical student, Hofmann soon reverted to his interests in Mormon documents and in forgery. In 1980 he 'discovered', neatly tucked into a copy of the King James Bible, a letter supposedly by the prophet Joseph Smith, in his 'reformed Egyptian' hieroglyphic hand, which according to some authorities went some way to confirming the truth of the Book of Mormon. Hofmann got $20,000 for it, and established his reputation.

He continued, for the next few years, to mine this rich seam of Mormon forgeries – he was both the coalminer and the coal – selling documents that were dangerous to the Mormon faith even more profitably than ones that appeared to confirm it. The major purchasers of this material were the Church of Jesus Christ of Latter-Day Saints in Utah and Missouri, who were gullible, rich, acquisitive and discreet. It's a tempting combination of attributes to a man like Hofmann. He had discovered within himself, he bragged, a capacity to 'menace and manipulate its leaders with nothing more sinister than a sheet of paper'. Anxious to get such stuff out of the public domain, the Mormon hierarchy were unprepared to come forward when questioned about their purchases, even after Hofmann was exposed.

But you can only 'discover' a limited number of new Mormon documents, and people were beginning to be suspicious of Hofmann. What could be more sensible than to expand his range? Over the next few years autographs from figures as diverse (and saleable) as John Quincy Adams, Daniel Boone, Mark Twain, John Hancock, Abraham Lincoln, Paul Revere and George Washington flowed from his pen and (like the Mormon material) fooled customers and experts alike.

Not enough, never enough. As the income poured in, expenditure rose alarmingly, as Hofmann and his wife soon began – a nice irony – to collect rare children's books, those emblems of nostalgic innocence. At the 1984 Antiquarian Book Fair in New York he began buying heavily from Justin Schiller, America's leading dealer in children's books, and a respected authority on bibliographic matters.

As both his income and his debts rose, Hofmann conceived the most ambitious of his projects, which, if successful, might well have netted him a million dollars. No copy of Hofmann's document had been located, though there was ample evidence that it had been printed, because various reprints occurred not long afterwards. So – unlike *Et Tu, Healy* – there was no need to seek (or to make up) the content: all you had to do was make up the object itself.

The content of Hofmann's audacious new project ran to a single page, and is known as the *Oath of a Freeman*, a Puritan document which was drafted in 1631 and first printed by Stephen Daye in 1639. No copy of this first printing has been located, though there are examples dated 1647 and 1649. It reads like this:

I, A. B. &c. being by the Almighty's most wise disposition become a member of this body, consisting of the Governor, Deputy Governor, Assistants and Commonalty of Massachusetts in New England, do freely and sincerely acknowledge that I am justly and lawfully subject to the Government of the same, and do accordingly submit my person and estate to be protected, ordered and governed by the laws and constitutions thereof, and do faithfully promise to be from time to time obedient and conformable thereunto, and to the authority of the said Governor and Assistants, and their successors, and to all such laws, orders, sentences and decrees as shall be lawfully made and published by them or their successors. And I will always endeavor (as in duty I am bound) to advance the peace and welfare of this body or commonwealth, to my utmost skill and ability. And I will, to my best power and means, seek to divert and prevent whatsoever may tend to ruin or damage thereof, or of any the said Governor, Deputy Governor, or Assistants, or any of them, or their successors, and will give speedy notice to them, or some of them, of any sedition, violence, treachery, or other hurt or evil, which I shall know, hear, or vehemently suspect, to be plotted or intended against the said commonwealth, or the said Government established. And I will not, at any time, suffer or give consent to any counsel or attempt, that shall be offered, given, or attempted, for the impeachment of the said Government, or making any change or alteration of the same, contrary to the laws and ordinances thereof; but shall do my utmost endeavor to discover, oppose and hinder all and every such counsel and attempt. So help me God.

This doesn't exactly trip off the tongue, but for an itinerant pilgrim in the 1630s, quivering with scripture and stricture, embarking upon a precarious new life amongst the savages and turkeys, it would have been pretty stirring stuff. Not because of what the oath maintains and requires, but because of what it omits.

Some 140 years later, the framers of the keystone document of American life spoke with similar confidence, though they wrote better prose: 'We hold these truths to be self-evident ... that all men are entitled to life, liberty, and the pursuit of happiness.' It sounds like a standard Enlightenment claim, but it sneaks in something relatively new ('the pursuit of happiness'?) and leaves out something large. *All men?* Unless, of course, they are brown. Or women. Never mind, everyone would have sort of understood that, and the more conditions you put into a proclamation, the more it's hedged about with exceptions and counter-examples, the less rhetorical power it has.

The *Oath of a Freeman* not only marks a seminal moment in American history; it would also (if a copy were found) be the first document printed in North America. It is highly significant historically because it is implicitly a document of revolution. It requires its free men to swear allegiance to God and to the Colony of Massachusetts, but *not* – striking in his absence – the king. And those, as would implicitly have been understood by all who swore to such an oath, those were fightin' words.

If Hofmann could produce an undetectable forgery, there was little question in his mind that he could get at least a million for it. Where to begin? Hofmann was fortunate – wise – in having chosen a document that might be presumed to have a stable text. Though individual printings, especially at this early date and with a tyro printer, always show subtle variations, there would be nothing to compare the 1639 *Oath* to. So, having been given the text, and a good look at its further printings only ten years after it first appeared, Hofmann had only the usual problems of paper, ink and design, which a sufficiently able forger might well be able to solve. But there was the problem of provenance. Where would Hofmann have found his copy, and where had it been all these years?

Easier the former than the latter. Hofmann made up a rough-and-ready, provisional forgery of something entitled *Oath of a Freeman*, which had nothing to do with the original Massachusetts document, and surreptitiously salted it away in a drawer full of obscure nineteenth-century broadsides at Argosy Bookshop in New York. It was a sensible choice of venue: Argosy is renowned for its enormous stock, and inexpensive material (such as Hofmann's ersatz broadside) would come and go without any of the sales staff being likely to remember either the piece or (even if they did) where it came from. On 23 March 1985, having extracted the broadside from the drawer into which he had just placed it, Hofmann purchased it (plus a few other unremarkable pieces) for $25 and asked for a handwritten receipt in which the title of each piece appeared. He was now the certified owner of a broadside entitled *Oath of a Freeman*.

All he had to do now was to introduce the *Oath* into the rare book world, but the problem was that he hadn't yet printed the 'real' thing. Another two weeks went by before he produced his document, at which point he informed his favourite dealer of the 'discovery'. The amiable Justin Schiller was an ideal foil: he had no reason to distrust the innocuous Hofmann, was anxious to retain him as a customer, and unlikely to conceive an immediate distrust of the broadside, which was out of field for him. When Hofmann suggested not merely that Schiller and his partner Raymond Wapner sell it on his behalf, but that they receive half the proceeds if it fetched over a million dollars (instead of the usual modest commission), he immediately had the dealers on, and at, his side. (The offer was too generous, and though it might have been construed as naïve, it should have set alarm bells ringing).

Schiller and Wapner were enormously excited by the discovery and its commercial possibilities, but also fully aware that authentication of the broadside would be a necessary and lengthy process and were anxious to make it transparent. With one proviso: Hofmann was unwilling to be named as the owner of the document. That it had been purchased by a private individual from Argosy Bookshop was acknowledged, and the receipt was offered as evidence, since it did not bear the buyer's name.

On 28 March, Wapner rang James Gilreath, a curator

at the Library of Congress, which was the obvious buyer and best repository for a document of such importance, to announce that he and Schiller had a copy of the *Oath* for sale 'at a price', which was eventually revealed as $1,500,000. The dealers insisted that all negotiations were to be confidential, and that it was up to the Library to satisfy itself with regard to authenticity. Some six weeks later, after exposing both the paper and ink to the usual rigorous tests, Gilreath announced that his investigators 'could find no evidence of forgery based on their examination of the material used to make the document'. This position, later misrepresented in the press as an 'authentication' of the document, merely confirmed that both ink and paper were consistent with the date of 1631, though no conclusion was drawn as to whether the ink had been *on* the paper since that date. But the report provided ample justification of Hofmann's later claim that he was 'a pretty good forger'.

Gilreath, shrewdly, was also pursuing another line of inquiry: he had been told, in conversation with Wapner, that the owner was a collector of children's books who lived in Utah. A few discreet inquiries later, and the name Mark Hofmann was on the table. Further inquiries in Utah revealed Hofmann as 'an untrustworthy person with suspicious friends', as well as the discoverer and seller of a considerable number of previously unknown Mormon documents.

Add to this disquieting provenance further doubts about title, and a great resistance to the price, and it was clear there was no deal, and on 5 June the Library of Congress withdrew its interest in purchasing the *Oath*. But Hofmann, with the curious innocence of the wicked, had rather assumed that the deal would go through, and begun to spend the proceeds. He bought a new house, and added to his bur-geoning book collection. He was able, though – being a con-vincing fellow – to talk the First International Bank of Salt Lake City into advancing him $185,000 as a loan against the alleged sale of the *Oath*, though the document had already been returned to Schiller and Wapner and was now on offer to the American Antiquarian Society, in Worcester, Massa-chusetts, a likely customer in view of the *Oath's* origin.

Early in September there was both good and bad news from the American Antiquarian Society. Like the Library of Congress, they could not offer proof that the document was a fake, and unlike the Library they were prepared to make an offer for it, subject to reasonable conditions. But that offer was only for $250,000, which, even if it was that little bit negotiable, was hardly likely to stretch to a million. On 11 September – that fateful day – the document was returned to New York, and Hofmann was informed that there was no buyer in the foreseeable future.

His response to this was remarkable, audacious and not as stupid as first appears. *He forged another copy.* He did not, of course, disclose this to his partners in New York. Instead, he found new partners (including his brother-in-law) in Salt Lake City. The receipt from Argosy could double as authen-tication for the second copy, and he could be frank about the fact that it had been on the market for over a million dollars. So long as neither of his partners knew about the other, it might just be possible to market two copies at the same time, under the pretence either that they were the same copy, or (his later version) that he had purchased a second copy from Argosy.

It was rather a fun plan, but it never came to fruition,

because the money ran out. Aside from forging his *Oath*, Hofmann had also been running what were in effect Ponzi schemes with rare books and manuscripts, soliciting investments which he then paid off with further money from new investors. It worked for a while, but now his creditors were closing in, and high-pitched salesmanship was no longer able to deter them.

It was time for Plan B: initiate some spectacular and eye-catching activity that might, for a time, divert attention from Hofmann and his collapsing home industry. It was time for murder. Why this would help is not clear. Perhaps it would simply take up a lot of police time, or maybe it would focus his creditors' minds on other things? But Hofmann convinced himself that anything was better than the humiliation of exposure, and was easily able to rationalise the forthcoming homicides. After all, he reasoned, 'my victims might die that day in a car accident or from a heart attack anyway.'

A month after he forged the second *Oath*, on 15 October 1985, Hofmann manufactured two pipe bombs, with which he murdered Steve Christensen and Kathleen Sheets. He had connections with both victims, but no particular animosity towards either: Christensen was a collector of documents and manuscripts, and the son of a prominent local businessman who had previously employed Kathleen Sheets. A day later, attempting to transport yet another bomb, it blew up and Hofmann was critically injured. Police attention, as you may imagine, immediately focused on him.

By now it was clear that Hofmann was not a mere bibliographic felon but a full-blown psychopath. The murders were the result of Hofmann's financial crisis, and he later claimed that if a sale to the American Antiquarian Society of

Massachusetts had realised a million dollars, he would not have killed his victims. Mark Hofmann pleaded guilty to his various crimes – he was initially charged with twenty-eight felonies – so his case never went to trial. He was convicted of the two murders, the forgery of a Mormon letter and the fraudulent sale of a fictional collection of manuscripts, but he was never charged with having forged the *Oath of a Freeman*. The copy offered through Justin Schiller never sold; the second one defrauded two Utah businessmen of $150,000. But there was no sense charging Hofmann with this crime when the sentences for the two murders would be much more severe. So we have the nice irony that the greatest forger of our time, eventually caught red-handed, was never punished for the most famous of his forgeries. He was sentenced to life imprisonment, and a parole board later confirmed that he should never be released.

Forgery is a recurring problem in the history of the rare book trade, for writers are amongst the very few professionals who can create an income with a stroke of the pen. Artists do this, of course, when they produce a drawing, as writers do when they write a book. But it is also a process that works spontaneously and casually, as Picasso might make a doodle on a napkin in a restaurant, or Hemingway might add a signature to a first edition. Hey presto: instant value! The wily George Bernard Shaw, recognising the value of his autograph in his years of fame, made sure to pay his local bills by cheque, knowing that many of the local tradesmen preferred his signature on a piece of paper to the few pounds that its encashment would bring.

In my years in the rare book trade I have encountered and rejected dozens of examples of forged signatures,

inscriptions and documents. Yet as sceptical and discrimi-
nating as one's eye becomes – and the eyes of those whom
one can consult when in doubt – there must have been other
phoney inscriptions and signatures that have evaded my
(our) attention. Last year a man from the south coast of
England was arrested for multiple forgeries of signatures
(purportedly by Hemingway, T. S. Eliot and others) in first
edition books. Most of them were competent if a little amateurish, and dealers soon began to pick them out. But less
knowledgeable buyers were fooled, in local auctions, on
eBay and on the rare book sites, and a lot of fraudulent
material was disseminated.

Aside from the handwriting, there are a number of possible indicators when you suspect a book inscription is a
forgery. If the inscription is by a major writer, it is of value
in itself, regardless of the value of the book in which it is
written. So you have to look carefully at which book it is in.
If you are going to forge, say, an Ian Fleming signature, it
would be stupid to buy a fine first edition of *Casino Royale*
in a dust wrapper (£25,000) to add a small percentage to its
value with an inscription. The rule is, buy a cheaper book
– a later book by Fleming without its dust wrapper – and
add a signature to that, thus transforming a £50 book into
a £1,500 one. If your Fleming signature is good enough,
and there have been some pretty good fakes on the market,
it must feel like free money, and the temptation to do more
will be irresistible.

But this leads, does it not, to a set of philosophical problems regarding the nature of identity? The teenage Mark
Hofmann, delightedly recognising that his altered collectable dimes were fooling even the experts, concluded that

there was therefore no problem. If it looked exactly the same, if it was under the most severe testing indistinguishable from the real thing, then it *was* the real thing. There was no difference save that of his own intervention: the difference now lay in the object's history and not its discernible nature.

Hofmann was, of course, kidding himself as well as others, and it turns out that his counterfeit dimes could in fact be identified and exposed. But what if they could not? What happens when you can produce a copy or facsimile of something that is genuinely indistinguishable from its original? Given the sophistication of modern techniques of reproduction, surely we can now produce copies of works of art – as well as dimes – that will pass even the most stringent test of authenticity?

How damaging this is depends on your cultural perspective. The Chinese, for instance, are said to treat copying as a form of homage to an original, and are apparently unworried by whether the ensuing object is by an original master or one of his admiring followers. In the Western tradition, too, major artists have often had workshops which employed skilled artisans, sometimes artists in their own right, to work on areas of a large painting, while happily later offering the picture as their own work. Art historians, knowing this, are still content to ascribe a painting to, say, Peter Paul Rubens, in the full knowledge that what counts as 'a Rubens' was often produced by multiple painters, of which he was occasionally the least active. Sometimes he only did the hands or faces.

What is it that we are excited by when we encounter a work of art? It cannot be simply 'the thing in itself' unless we are prepared either to accept that a perfect copy of the *Mona Lisa* is just as satisfactory as the real thing, or alternatively that the notion of the artistic object has to include *as part of its definition* its own history? The real *Mona Lisa* is preferable to a perfect copy because it was painted by Leonardo, and the fact that it is, is part of our response to it. In this sense, then, provenance is an *essential* aspect of the aesthetic experience, not something added to it. Take that away, and what looks as if it were the same thing feels pale and diminished.

The curious implication of this is that, in order to frame an 'aesthetic' response to a work of art, we need to know whether it is genuine or not. If I put before you – allow me this hypothetical – not one but two *Mona Lisas* which are *identical* (except that only one of them is by Leonardo), you would rightly admire them, on close examination, equally. Once it was revealed that picture 'A' was a copy and 'B' was the original, you would have no *aesthetic* reason to prefer the one to the other. But you would, and rightly, though it would be hard to defend this decision if the pictures were, as it were, shuffled, and you no longer knew which was which.

'I love the one that is by Leonardo,' you would say, 'whichever it is. And I admire the copy, but it is an inferior thing. Not by virtue of its appearance, but of its history.'

It's an unsettling conclusion, but I see no way to avoid it.

6

Auto da Fé: The Burning of the *Memoirs* of Lord Byron

In the autumn of 2003 I was asked by the Tate Gallery Archive to appraise some material they had been offered for sale, consisting largely of sketchbooks by the painter John Piper, which were housed at John Murray Publishers on Albemarle Street in central London. I accepted as a matter of course, though without much hope that I would enjoy it, as I find most of Piper's evocations of churches, ruins and land-scapes watery and romanticised, redolent of the most boring and sentimental 'Englishness'. Piper may be regarded as an antidote to Sutherland – not much thorny obfuscation in his natural world – but that is hardly enough to recommend him. I prefer Sutherland, who at least provides images that demand close attention, and are worth arguing with.

I had never visited Murray's Albemarle Street premises, which are amongst the oldest, most famous – indeed, most celebrated – of all English publishing houses. The present John Murray and his capable and charming wife, Virginia, were the seventh generation of Murrays to run the company, which was founded in 1768, and which continued to operate from Albemarle Street for nearly two centuries. Though it is often said that the building was purchased with the proceeds from *Childe Harold*, in fact Murray put up his three most valuable copyrights as a guarantee: Mrs Rundell's cookery book, Scott's *Marmion* and the *Quarterly Review*. For several generations John Murray published many, you might even argue most, of the greatest writers and thinkers of the eighteenth and nineteenth centuries: Thomas Malthus, Lord Byron, Sir Walter Scott, Jane Austen, Charles Darwin, David Livingstone, Herman Melville. The list goes on and on.

Before I was shown down to the basement, where the Piper sketchbooks resided, there was ample time – it seemed as if there was always ample time with the Murrays, nothing was rushed, nor were cordialities compressed and perfunctory – for a chat. This was more than a result of impeccable manners, though it was certainly an example of them; rather, it was an exposure to a house style that had pertained, in this very house, for many generations of distinctly gentlemanly publishing. Mr and Mrs Murray showed me into the front room on the first floor, which overlooks Albemarle Street, a pleasingly proportioned if unexceptional Georgian drawing room of a genteel rather than grand sort, with a fireplace on the left hand wall. It was a warm summer's day, and no fire blazed comfortingly in the hearth, though it was easy enough – it was virtually obligatory – to imagine Jane Austen or Charles Darwin warming themselves in front of it on a chilly winter's afternoon. But this fireplace – if a fireplace could be called 'notorious', this would merit the appellation – was not the cosy hearth which the usual stereotypes demand.

'You know, of course, what happened here,' said Mr Murray, without the slightest question at the end of the sentence.

The late Jock Murray standing in front of the fireplace in which
Lord Byron's *Memoirs* were burnt.

I did. On 17 May 1824 the manuscript of two volumes of Lord Byron's *Memoirs* were burned in this very fireplace. And I felt impelled, looking into that inoffensive fire grate, to make some leap of imagination, to see the flames, the paper warming, beginning to singe, then to burn, and eventually to give off the light of active conflagration. To try to reconstruct with what mixture of emotions the men round the fireplace would have gazed upon those dwindling pages, as their decision to consign the manuscript to oblivion became irreversible.

But it was quite impossible, on that sunny day, the room warm and bathed in light, imaginatively to reconstruct what Byron's biographer Fiona MacCarthy has called 'the most famous sacrificial scene in literary history', an overstatement that is somehow appropriate to the Byron legend, in which everything is written in bold, and of the utmost consequence.

The death of one manuscript by fire brings to mind the death of many others, for there is a long tradition of great literary work perishing amongst the flames. Often the author himself is responsible for the destruction, the burning of a manuscript being an old-fashioned way of pushing the Delete button. James Joyce burned a play and the first sections of *Stephen Hero* (some of the pages were rescued from the fire by his brother), while Gerard Manley Hopkins burned many of his early poems. There seems nothing wrong with either of these acts – and many like them – for it is a writer's prerogative to distinguish what they wish to transmit from what, for whatever reason, they do not. That's their job.

The troubles arise when the act of destruction is done by

someone else. Frequently it happens through executors or relatives anxious to protect the reputation of the author and/ or the feelings of their relations. The Marquis de Sade's son burned all of his father's many unpublished works, following his death, though it is hard to imagine that the Marquis had much reputation left to protect. One might well feel the same about Richard Burton's widow's destruction of the surviving manuscript translation of *The Perfumed Garden,* the sort of Eastern erotica which now seems rather tame, with which he will always be associated. More intriguingly, the relatives of Lewis Carroll, known for his sexualised photographs of little girls, destroyed four volumes of his diaries, perhaps ensuring that his reputation, though compromised by the survival of these images, was not undermined entirely by more revealing material.

The two volumes of the Byron *Memoirs* were burned by a group of his friends and executors after three days of feverish comings and goings following the poet's death, during which few of them made an effort actually to read the material. By some accounts, a quick look through the contents was enough to convince the majority that – given what was already known about Byron's proclivities and activities – the material could not be published. Their disapprobation may have been justified – who knows? – but the fact that the work was deemed unpublishable seems scant reason to burn it. There seems something punitive about this over-response, as if the papers were being consigned to damnation.

Unlike the diaries of Philip Larkin, which were destroyed at his own wish, Byron's *Memoirs* were intended for publication and were burned, one supposes, in order to respect the reputation of others, largely women, whose names (if

remembered at all) we recall now only because of their association with Byron. Minor Regency aristocrats, catapulted
into specious immortality because they were lovers of the
'mad, bad and dangerous to know' Byron. Indeed, Caroline
Lamb's description of him is virtually all we remember of
her.

So who cares if the work would have exposed more lovers
and illicit acts, more peccadilloes, more cavalier and caddish
escapades? Surely there was little that could add to the
myth of Byron, and the worse the behaviour and incidents
recorded, the more, well, Byronic Byron becomes.

We'd quite like him to be worse. It's a reasonable enough
desire, but unfortunately there is little convincing evidence
that the contents were sensational, which makes the question
of why they were destroyed even more puzzling. Byron's
Memoirs, unlike Larkin's diaries, were not in any sense
private. The two people who had a glance at the Larkin
volumes were agreed that they were intensely and unpleas-
antly self-revealing, and that there would be no great loss to
literature if they were destroyed. But Byron didn't merely
envisage the posthumous publication of his *Memoirs*; he
had offered an early look at them to those people whom
he termed 'the elect' – a category that, curiously, did not
include his most intimate friend, and one of his literary
executors, John Cam Hobhouse, who was deeply offended
by his omission from that exalted category, and whose subsequent attitude to the fate of the *Memoirs* – burn! – may well
have been an expression of this pique.

Byron died in Missolonghi, in western Greece, on the
evening of 19 April 1824, at the age of thirty-six. It took
almost a month for the news to reach England, a period in

which Greece went into a paroxysm of national mourning. The poet was revered in his adopted land, which he had led in its fight for independence against the Turks. But Byron was increasingly reviled at home, his decision to live abroad taken as proof of guilt. The obituary notice in *John Bull*, on 16 May, was not atypical of this mood:

> He has ... quitted the world at the most unfortunate period of his career, and in the most unsatisfactory manner – in voluntary exile, when his mind, debased by evil associations, and the malignant brooding over imaginary ills, has been devoted to the construction of elaborate lampoons.

His embalmed body was returned to England, though legend has it that his lungs and larynx remained in Greece, to be buried like the relics of a saint. In England there were calls for him to be interred in Westminster Abbey, which were refused on the grounds of his 'questionable morality', and it wasn't until 145 years had passed that a memorial plaque was set there in his honour.

John Galt, a snobbish and obtuse early biographer, conveyed pretty accurately the image of Byron that was to pertain in the years after his death, as his reputation as a poet began to wane:

> It would have been wonderful had he proved an amiable and well-conducted man, than the questionable and extraordinary being who has alike provoked the malice and interested the admiration of the world. Posterity, while acknowledging the eminence of his endowments, and lamenting the habits which his unhappy circumstances

induced, will regard it as a curious phenomenon in the fortunes of the individual, that the progress of his fame as a poet should have been similar to his history as a man.

Which is to say, a bit of a rotter, justly forgotten. It's no wonder that his executors and close associates had tried to preserve what was good of him, and to burn the rest.

The volumes of his *Memoirs* were never read by the three main players in the ensuing drama: Augusta Leigh, Byron's half-sister, Lady Byron and his publisher John Murray. The two women, of course, had much to hide from public scrutiny, though their 'secrets' were commonplaces of contemporary gossip: Augusta Leigh had an incestuous relationship with her half-brother, while Lady Byron's separation from her husband was, indeed, because he was mad, bad and dangerous to know, and the possibility of sensational divulgations loomed. There were suggestions that Byron had attempted 'unspeakable intimacies' with his wife, code at the time for buggery. The allegations were almost certainly true – no one intimate with Lord Byron was likely to rise *ano intacto* – but which he heatedly denied, for the act was regarded not merely as an abomination but was punishable by law.

In a gentlemanly spirit of conciliation, the poet had offered Lady Byron a chance to read the material, which she, fearing that even an edited version would then bear her imprimatur, had declined to do. After the manuscript was destroyed, however, her response was more equivocal than might have been expected by those friends of hers who thought themselves to be protecting her interests:

I do concur *now* in the expediency and propriety of the

destruction, but had the question been *then* submitted to me, they certainly would not have been consumed by *my* decision. It is therefore perhaps as well it was not.

John Murray, too, had been in a difficult situation. The *Memoirs* had been gifted by Byron to his friend the Irish poet Thomas Moore in 1819, on the clear understanding that he might choose to sell them. They were undoubtedly valuable property, and when Moore sold them to Byron's publisher in November 1821, he received 2,000 guineas (roughly equivalent to £180,000 now, which, while it seems a lot, is certainly a lot less than James Patterson will get as an advance for his next novel).

Murray would have known that, even at the price, he was still likely to be onto a large profit. But even this potential gain was not enough to convince him to actually read the manuscript. Byron's previous works, especially *Cain* and (his masterpiece) *Don Juan* had scandalised those readers who devour shocking material and then publicly disavow it. The likelihood, then, is that Murray, who was increasingly uneasy about Byron's output, had decided not to publish before buying the *Memoirs*. I presume he conceived himself to be ensuring against some other firm publishing them, and thus safeguarding Byron's posthumous reputation.

Yet Murray's attitude was curious, for Byron had written to him in October 1819 to offer him a chance to read the manuscript, with the assurance that

> I have left out all my *loves* (except in a general way) and many other of the most important things (because I must not compromise other people), so that it is like the play of

Hamlet – 'the part of Hamlet omitted by particular desire'.
But you will find many opinions, and some fun.

Though he admitted to having given 'a detailed account of my marriage and its consequence', he apparently regarded his account as fair comment. It included, according to one reader of the manuscript, an account of the poet making love to his wife on the sitting-room settee on their wedding day. But he was confidently unrepentant: 'I cannot pretend to be impartial, no, by the Lord, not while I feel.'

Of the 'elect' who had in fact read the manuscript, opinions differed. Most found it relatively unobjectionable – Lord John Russell finding only 'three or four pages … too gross and indelicate for publication' – though Hobhouse noted in his journal that 'Gifford of the *Quarterly* who read it at Murray's request said the whole *Memoirs* were only fit for a brothel and would damn Lord B. to everlasting infamy.' This cannot have been entirely accurate, for by most accounts the erotic escapades were all to be found in the second volume.

Surely the presence of such salacious material would add little to our image of Byron? But its absence titillates and provokes speculation that something genuinely new and sensational might just have been revealed. The absence of the diaries casts a beguiling shadow across the Byron myth, and tantalises us with possible untold stories, extra badness.

On 17 May the six principals in the decision to burn the *Memoirs* met in Murray's office, soon to be joined by his son, all of them warmed by the fire that was soon to engulf the offending manuscript. The party was by no means unanimous in its conclusion: Hobhouse and Murray were keen for the coming conflagration, though the publisher had previously suggested that the volumes be returned to Byron's half-sister (a further suggestion that they be placed in the hands of 'some banker' was also rejected); Thomas Moore and Henry Luttrell, both of whom had actually read the material, argued for its preservation; Wilmot Horton and Colonel Doyle, there to represent what they conceived to be Lady Byron's interests, were mildly inclined to side with Murray and Hobhouse. After an hour's discussion, and what Hobhouse described as 'a good deal of squabbling', hotter heads prevailed, and Horton and Doyle consigned the pages to the flames.

Yet even if one sympathises with the decision to protect the world from this potentially explosive material, there surely were other ways to act. The problem with burning something, as Joan of Arc might have observed, is that you can't take it back. Might they not have been published in some expurgated form? An even better result would simply have been to preserve the material, keep it in a safe place in the firm's archives, and in the fullness of time – perhaps a great deal of time – look at the issue again.

That, after all, is what archives can be for: for tucking stuff away until the time is right for someone to take a proper look at it. Sometimes material that is potentially private or controversial can, on agreement, be placed under seal for a certain period of time. The Murray archive, which has since the earliest days been kept with considerable diligence, eventually came to house almost all of Byron's manuscripts and letters to his publisher, but also a great deal more. Hobhouse inherited a mass of Byron papers following the author's death in 1824, as well as having his own letters from the poet. All of this material was eventually bequeathed to Murray's, as well as further substantial material from a number of Lord Byron's closest friends. From such sources came not merely manuscripts and letters but a vast array of personal memorabilia: further portraits, clothes, medals and a host of incoming letters from swooning women admirers and former lovers, many of whom sent tresses of their hair, which the poet duly packaged individually. All of the manuscripts were included in the sale, in 2005, of the Murray archive to the National Library of Scotland for the much-discussed, and frequently criticised, price of £31 million (which seemed a bargain to me).

George Gordon, Lord Byron – *the Byron of myth and legend* – was born on 23 March 1812. He was twenty-four at the time. Oh, he'd been around before then, and was a well-known and respected, independently wealthy man about town, a promising author and (reputedly) bon viveur. But following the publication and unanticipated success of the first two Cantos of *Childe Harold's Pilgrimage*, he observed, some three days later: 'I awoke one morning and found myself famous.' Not famous as in extremely well known. Famous in a new way, which carried with it a hint of infamy too. Famous as in celebrated, dreamed of, fantasised about, feared and admired, the kind of notoriety that makes women swoon and their husbands clench their fists, or sphincters. The kind of fame that thrills: 'Byronic'. There are few comparable adjectives in our literary lexicon that carry the same weight or resonance. 'Orwellian' casts a deep shadow, but 'Byronic' rearranges the light.

Contemporary portraits of the poet, the most famous of which were done in the few years succeeding the success of *Childe Harold*, show an idealised figure, already indistinguishable from how he was widely imagined. Richard Holmes's description catches the figure perfectly: 'The large head with its dark curls, mocking eyes and voluptuous mouth distracted from the stocky body that was always tending to overweight and the distinctive limp with its hint of the cloven hoof. He was Apollo combined with Mephistopheles.'

He was ravishing, as irresistible as a force of nature: being in his presence, Coleridge noted in a letter of 1816, was like seeing the sun. In the famous Richard Westall image of 1813 (which hangs in the National Portrait Gallery in London) a highly sensitive Byron is turned to the right, showing a thoughtful profile as his chin rests in his hand. He is pouting slightly, as if some pleasure were denied or merely contemplated, and his hand seems enlarged, as if it could grasp whatever it desired. His lips are full and deeply coloured – anticipating the even redder lips in portraits by Thomas Phillips (1814), James Holmes and G. H. Harlow (both 1815), in which the lips are so red as to suggest the application of artistic licence, or of lipstick. It is hard to find the equivalent until we come to some of the memorable images of Marilyn Monroe.

This is Byron as he would have wished, and was widely conceived, to look, but there is evidence against any portrait of him – as these all are – as a sensitive sensualist. He was disposed, we know, to run to fat: no one with his imperious desires could have been lacking in appetite. Fearing the worst, he had himself weighed regularly on the scales made available to anxious gentlemen of portly disposition at the St James' wine merchants Berry Bros and Rudd. At eighteen years old he had ballooned up to almost fourteen stone (his height is variously estimated at between five feet eight inches and six feet), and with his congenital deformity, often mis-described as 'a club foot', he was largely unable to take the requisite exercise. Instead, on going up to Cambridge, he dieted. Fasted is perhaps a better term – his biographer Fiona MacCarthy actually describes him as 'anorexic' – for a regime that consisted largely of biscuits, soda water and potatoes soaked in vinegar, which he believed would not only slim him down but also sharpen his mind.

It seems to have worked. Within five years he had lost some five stone, produced a great deal of poetry and could certainly report undiminished sexual desire, and success. His most famous conquest, Lady Caroline Lamb, was besotted with him, and when Byron eventually cast her adrift, she languished, wept and diminished, causing him cruelly to observe that he was being 'haunted by a skeleton'.

After leaving England he continued this extreme self-denial, eating bread, tea and vegetables, with an occasional weak spritzer, though he was later to acknowledge that his dieting (and perhaps the constant cigars that he used as a substitute for food) was 'the cause of more than half our maladies'. An anonymous amateurish portrait of him done in 1822, still revealing his left profile, reveals, with the integrity of a Graham Sutherland, the truth of an emaciated and unhappy man, haunted by his *own* skeleton, in poignant contrast to the pictures of him less than ten years earlier, of the heady few years of fame and notoriety following the publication of *Childe Harold*.

It is hard, quite, to explain the impact of that poem. It opens particularly badly:

Not in those climes where I have late been straying,
Though Beauty long hath there been matchless deemed
…

The reader might suppose its author both metrically and
physically lame-footed. The lines are almost impossible to
recite without faltering and gagging, and the rest of the
poem, though intermittently witty and engaging, is mostly
long-winded pedestrian stuff, as darkly unappealing as its
hero himself.

Childe Harold is a high-born, relentlessly self-referring
young man, and his pilgrimage is clearly an autobiographical
travelogue (the hero was originally called Burun). On leaving
England to see something of the world, Harold is 'more restless than the swallow in the skies', as the poem badly puts it.
(Are swallows 'restless'?) He has embarked on these travels
because of some unspecified 'crime' – of the kind, perhaps,
of which Byron himself was frequently accused: incest?
buggery? paedophilia? – which has sundered him from the
only woman whom he has loved and rendered him, like Coleridge's Ancient Mariner, isolated and bereft:

And now I'm in the world alone,
Upon the wide, wide sea;
But why should I for others groan,
When none will sigh for me?

But they did, they did. In the days following publication
of the first *Cantos*, Byron was besieged by female admirers, anxious that he be alone no more. Carriages drew up,
invitations arrived, beseeching notes were written. Already

with some well-deserved reputation as a *roué*, all of a sudden Byron became the most sought-after man, not merely in England, but in Europe.

For a while, anyway. Tempestuous storms of this hysterical sort pass quickly enough and often leave in their wake bitterness and regret. Within a couple of years Byron, once so assiduously courted, was widely reviled in England, accused of many things, none of them specified, quite, and all the more fascinating as a result. He was encouraged, like Oscar Wilde later, to leave England immediately and, unlike Oscar, had the sense to do so. He left in 1816, still a figure of mystery and overweening attractiveness on the continent, never to return to his homeland.

But first he had to kit himself out properly, in a manner not only befitting his established image but likely to embellish it considerably. Always dandified in dress and manner, he made certain that he would be noticed wherever he went. He travelled from Brussels to Italy in a 'monumental' black carriage, containing his bed, as well as a travelling library, silver and china. His biographer puts it crisply: 'Drawn by four or six horses, it was nothing less than a small palatial residence on wheels.' Byron could certainly not afford the outlay for this magnificent vehicle, and at the time of his death still owed the £500 to Baxter, his coach-maker.

Who, one wonders, did he think he was? A king? No, not good enough: there were dozens of kings dotted about, some of them a bit seedy. It was common to be a king. No, he thought of himself as an Emperor, *the* Emperor. He thought of himself as a sort of Napoleon-lite: 'I don't know – but I think, *I*, even *I* (an insect compared with this creature), have set my life on casts not a millionth part of this man's.'

He wrote odes to his hero, collected memorabilia and suffered during his defeats. Such psychic identification can have disastrous consequences. It was no doubt with his Napoleonic hero in mind that Byron embarked on his military campaigns – about which he knew almost nothing – in Greece, and which might be claimed to have led indirectly to his death. It was an inglorious end, and might easily have been avoided had his doctors, with their obsessive blood-letting, simply allowed him to get some rest and gradually recuperate from debilitating fever and infection.

His hero-worship of Napoleon, and emulation of him, however, were saved from mere preposterousness by that most telling of all Byron's intellectual virtues, irony and self-mockery: 'with me there is, as Napoleon said, but one step between the sublime and the ridiculous.' He and his hero were, he averred wryly, 'the two greatest examples of vanity … in the present age'.

Byron spent eight years on the continent, a period into which he packed more incident, personal relationships and literary composition than most men can produce in a life-time, living with such intensity that you might have supposed him to be anticipating a premature death. He had, after all, the examples both of his friend Shelley, and of Keats, both dead in their twenties.

Lord Byron died at the age of thirty-six, a hero amongst the Greeks, revered in Europe, a figure, still, of twitchy fascination in his native land. An early death was a good career decision, as it is hard to imagine Byron in old age, his powers of every sort waning, no longer the swashbuckling figure of a gilded youth. His poetical work is uneven, filled with bombast and unreadable verse drama, and if he is still read today outside the university syllabus and the ranks of the Byronists, it is for a few anthologisable lyrics, and the delightful *Don Juan,* which scandalised his publisher, who found its 'approximations to indelicacy' so offensive that he eventually declined to publish the later Cantos (of which there were sixteen, and an unfinished seventeenth).

A rambling picaresque satire tracing the career of its much-seduced (rather than seducing) hero, *Don Juan* reminds us that Byron, at his best, seems to have more in common with Pope than with his putative fellow 'Romantics'. By this time in his life he was increasingly dismissive of Wordsworth, Coleridge, Southey and Leigh Hunt, and it is certainly harder, and less rewarding, to enumerate the similarities between Byron and Wordsworth than their manifold differences. Certainly none of his contemporaries could have written with such wit, daring and panache, and if he had written little else (one sometimes wishes he had written *less*), his place in world literature would be assured.

In this respect, though, he is typical of the Romantic poets – perhaps of all poets – in that his reputation rests upon a slight percentage of his oeuvre, from which a lot of indifferent stuff must be excused. Most of Wordsworth is dross, Keats was still learning his trade, much of Shelley makes one cringe, Coleridge could profitably be condensed into twenty pages. But Byron is luminous in a way that his contemporaries were not, and that is partly because of the life, and the myths that he self-consciously engendered.

In this he recalls Oscar Wilde (who revered Byron) in so many ways: as author, dandy, aesthete, wit, bisexual libertine. Both flouted convention yet were in thrall to public opinion, hence the ironised self-aggrandisement. Each died at a tragically early age, a victim of his own nature. But the differences are crucial: Wilde wanted to be famous, Byron wanted to be a hero. It is impossible to imagine Oscar as a soldier (though he would have loved flouncing about in uniform), quite inconceivable to imagine him actually fighting. He would have sympathised with – and then used as his own – the aesthete Ernest Thesiger's later great quip about his service at the front during the First World War: 'My dear, the *noise!* And the *people!*' Byron would have revelled in both.

But for both writers the life became a work of art. Famous for being famous, like our contemporary two-bit celebrities? Certainly not. Byron and Wilde were celebrated not merely for the outward show, but because they produced work that continues to amuse, provoke and delight. And, by a further and final irony, in both cases the work for which they should be remembered occurred in the byways and interstices of their literary output. Wilde was an essayist of the highest quality, whose writings on art, life, literature and beauty are abidingly fascinating. And Byron is now most memorable for his letters and journals, which throb and hum with vibrant life. He is one of the great masters of the craft. I suspect he would have been a great memoirist, too, had those two volumes not burned in that fireplace at his misguided publishers on Albemarle Street.

7

A Matter of Life and Death: The Diaries of Philip Larkin

It's hard to claim that the dashing Lord Byron and the retiring Philip Larkin, who couldn't have swashbuckled his own raincoat, had much in common. Byron's life was an overt and passionate testimony to his values – or lack of them – whereas Larkin led an apparently innocuous existence squirrelled away in the Brynmor Jones Library at Hull University, whinging occasionally and producing a small and exquisite body of poems. But when you peel back the apparent dissimilarities, parallels begin to emerge. Both, after a period of high esteem, had their reputations severely challenged, and in both cases intimate works of self-revelation were destroyed upon, or nearly upon, their deaths.

Like Byron, Philip Larkin was adored by his friends. 'The funniest man I've ever known', said his editor at Faber and Faber, Charles Monteith; 'the best company of anyone I have met', agreed his chum and posthumous editor the poet Anthony Thwaite. Playful, puckish, self-deprecating, a terrific mimic and a natural entertainer, the private Larkin seemed anything but a librarian on leave. As if out on day-release, he seemed determined to be naughty. In his letters and conversation he often defined himself in terms of his dislikes. He was rude about most of his fellow poets, had a near phobia about foreign travel, hated the democratising and lowering effects of modern politics, seemed to despise the new immigrants to British society, cringed at the thought of the mass of humans going about their lives.

He lived in a permanent state of fastidious recoil. Even his jokey persona with his friends was based on ironising and dramatising his dislikes. He was never funnier than when he was loathing something. But though the range of his disapproval was panoptic, there was only one thing that he both detested and feared, and that was death. Not death generally – he could contemplate the large-scale destruction of his fellow man with an equanimity approaching satisfaction. No, what he could not abide was the thought of his own demise.

At the age of twenty-nine, though he retained some of that youthful insouciance that regards death as something that happens to other people, Larkin was intrigued by the subject:

To me, death is the most important thing about life (because it puts an end to life and extinguishes further hope of restitution or recompense, as well as any more experience) ... I know it might be said that death is about as important as the final whistle in a football match that ... it is what happens before that matters. True, but after a football match there are other football matches; after death there's nothing. I don't think death can be compared to anything in life, since it is by its nature entirely unlike.

This feels literary and second-hand, uninfected by personal

Larkin and his lover Monica Jones dressing up and enjoying life.

anxiety. But only nine years later, still a relatively young man, he got a whiff of the thing in itself, and was utterly cowed.

Admitted to hospital, in March 1961, with a variety of unsettling symptoms ('there is something wrong with my vision ... & I feel rather distant from my feet: all this is summed up by being *aware* of my right eye'), he wrote a plaintive, meandering letter to his lover Monica Jones, stuffed with terrified foreboding and an overwhelming desire to flee: 'I *dread* hospitals, & the very phrase "results of the x ray" makes my blood run cold.' Fearful as a result of these ill-defined, rather surreal symptoms, he suspects cancer of the brain. Or maybe of the liver. Or flu, perhaps.

Castigating himself continually – 'I'm really a horrible coward ... I'm rigid with funk ... how awful this all is' – Larkin has a confession, and an apology, to make. It was wrong, he acknowledges and regrets, not to have allowed Monica access to his flat while he was in hospital. The reason he gives is both revealing and guarded:

> I had left a few private papers & diaries lying around. Such things, which I suppose I keep partly for the record in the event of wanting to write an autobiography, & partly to relieve my feelings, will have to be burned unread in the event of my death, & I couldn't face anyone I thought had seen them, let alone being willing to expose you or anyone else to the embarrassment of & no doubt even pain of reading what I had written.

What's that all about, then? Larkin was, even at this relatively early stage of his life, quite open and jokey about his politically incorrect (as they were not yet called) opinions, and his relationship with Monica was certainly frank. In the voluminous correspondence between them – there are over 2,000 letters (now at the Bodleian Library in Oxford) from Larkin to her – he was generally candid. Indeed, the letter I have quoted, full of funk and self-dislike, is not at all concerned to make a good impression, to feign optimism or courage, to mask his anxieties for the sake of Monica's peace of mind. It makes you wonder what the journals contained.

His conclusion about the status and fate of them, though, is a little ambiguous: 'What this will lead me to do about such things in the future I don't know – assuming there is a future. Perhaps destroy them right away.' Does 'right away' mean right *now*? Or 'right away' in that future, on knowing death to be imminent? Whichever meaning you choose, though, one thing is certain: no one must read them, ever. Which makes you wish you could.

Larkin's terror regarding death – it was nothing less – didn't abate, as one might have assumed, or at least hoped, as time went by and the inevitable approached. One of his most successful poems, 'Aubade', tackles the subject directly:

> I work all day, and get half-drunk at night.
> Waking at four to soundless dark, I stare.
> In time the curtain-edges will grow light.
> Till then I see what's really always there:
> Unresting death, a whole day nearer now,
> Making all thought impossible but how
> And where and when I shall myself die.
> Arid interrogation: yet the dread
> Of dying, and being dead,
> Flashes afresh to hold and horrify.

During the course of his final illness in 1985 the prospect of imminent death was constantly (in spite of reassurance from his doctors) in his mind. Letters written in his last months to Kingsley Amis, Robert Conquest, Blake Morrison and Andrew Motion have a wry, mordant tone, certainly distinguishable from the frantic anxiety of his early letter to Monica from hospital. Six weeks before he died, he wrote to Motion: 'I have an uneasy suspicion that the curtain is about to go up on Act II of the Larkin Drama – not well, tiresome symptoms, call in the quacks. So brush up on your Shovel and Headstone: Duties of Executors.'

It was time to put his house in order, but he lacked the will to do so. His health declined, he lost appetite and weight, and, though he continued to visit the doctor, his hopes of recovery were fading. Three days before his death he asked Betty Mackereth, his secretary (and lover), 'to destroy my diaries'. She did so immediately; after first taking off the covers to preserve them, she fed the thirty volumes into a shredder, and then (for good measure) incinerated the strips of shredded paper. Within hours, the documents that – one imagines – most explicitly revealed the inner life, or at least the most guarded secrets (which is something different), of one of the twentieth century's great poets were no more.

Mackereth had no compunction about what she had done. She had followed Philip's fervent final wish: 'He was quite clear about it: he wanted them destroyed. I didn't read them as I put them in the machine, but I couldn't help seeing little bits and pieces. They were very unhappy. Desperate really.'

I wonder why Larkin didn't do it himself. Perhaps it would have felt like a form of suicide? Philip Roth is good on this topic: 'It takes more courage than one might imagine to destroy … secret diaries … to obliterate forever the relic-like force of those things that, almost alone of our possessions, decisively answer the question: Can it really be that I am like this?'

Larkin died early on Monday morning, 2 December, remarking faintly to the nurse who was holding his hand at his bedside, 'I am going to the inevitable', which feels admirably studied, as if his last moments were spent in considering and honing this final line. Presumably his trip to the inevitable was eased when it was confirmed to him that the diaries were no more.

It is hard to question the wisdom of obeying a dying man's last request. Yet many commentators have wondered whether it was right to have acceded to Larkin's wish. To get this into perspective, we may recall the analogous, and much more consequential, case of Franz Kafka, who left instructions to destroy all of his unpublished manuscripts, which his friend Max Brod chose to ignore. As a result, we have some of the great novels of the twentieth century.

But the differences between the cases are obvious. Kafka asked for the destruction to be done after his death, so he could never confirm that his wishes had been carried out. And it was clear, even at that moment, that works of high importance to Western literature were at risk if the instruction were to be carried out. There is a nice, almost a classical, conflict of duties here. Should Brod keep his word and honour his friend's wishes, or break his word and honour his friend's genius?

The key lies in the nature and importance of what would have been lost, and who is to decide. Byron's executors made their decision ostensibly on his behalf, which seems to me reprehensible, though without a hint of what the *Memoirs* contained it is hard to know if even Byron might finally have concurred with their decision. So when we return to the case of Larkin, we have to ask: how important were these diaries in themselves, and to our understanding of Larkin as man and artist? Were they sufficiently significant that an intimate friend would have been justified in lying to him about having destroyed them?

Various friends have speculated about their contents. Jean Hartley, who with her husband, George, published Larkin's seminal collection *The Less Deceived,* believed that they revealed Larkin at his bitchiest and most coruscating towards those closest to him. Larkin's biographer Andrew Motion notes that the 'diaries function as sexual log-books, and a gigantic repository for bile, resentment, envy and misanthropy'. The disapproving tone here is found on a regular basis in Motion's generally sympathetic account of Larkin, which led to Martin Amis's unimprovable rejoinder: 'In Andrew Motion's book, we have the constant sense that Larkin is somehow falling short of the cloudless emotional health enjoyed by, for instance, Andrew Motion.' This is gorgeously dismissive, but its showy assurance masks a real problem. Larkin liked being offensive, or at the very least, larking about with extreme right-wing, misogynist and racist ideas. He revelled in it.

Following the publication of the Larkin *Letters* in 1992, various critics were duly offended. Tom Paulin, who has deep reserves of indignation, put the case clearly, describing the contents as 'a distressing and in many ways revolting compilation which imperfectly reveals and conceals the sewer under the national monument Larkin became'. Joining the chorus of disapprobation, Professor Lisa Jardine, of the University of London, described their author as a 'casual, habitual racist and an easy misogynist', observing with some pleasure that 'we don't tend to teach Larkin much now in my department of English. The Little Englandism he celebrates sits uneasily within our revised curriculum.' Even Alan Bennett, himself capable of a bit of smutty puckishness, remarked that Larkin looked a bit like a rapist, and noted unsettling resemblances to John Reginald Halliday Christie, the Rillington Place serial killer.

Over-reactions? Perhaps Bennett goes too far, but there is a lot to be uneasy, and queasy, about. Instances of Larkin at his most objectionable are not hard to come by, either in the letters or (unpublished during his lifetime) occasional verses. He regularly composed little squibs to amuse his chums, of which the following song, written in 1970, is typical (I cite it because I once, a little uneasily, sold the manuscript):

> Prison for strikers,
> Bring back the cat,
> Kick out the niggers –
> What about that?
> (Chorus: niggers, niggers, etc.)
> Trade with the Empire,
> Ban the obscene,
> Lock up the Commies,
> God save the Queen
> (Chorus: commies, commies, etc.)

This is so perfect a rendition of the attitudes of the Little-Englanders that Professor Jardine complains of, that you might suppose it a parody. But there is just too much of this stuff, spread throughout the entire corpus of both poetry and correspondence. It frequently occurs as light verse, but is just as likely, and far more tellingly, to be interjected into an otherwise inoffensive letter, as if a momentarily repressed rage just had to find its way out. Thus an otherwise amiable and chatty letter to Colin Gummer, in September 1984, ends with a description of a visit to Lord's (Larkin loved cricket) and builds foam as it goes:

> I don't mind England not beating the West Indies ... And as for those black scum kicking up a din on the boundary – a squad of South African police would have sorted them out to my satisfaction.
>
> I survey the national scene with a kind of horrified fascination. Scargill & Co. can't lose: either they get what they are asking for or they reduce the country to chaos, at which point their friends the Russkis come marching in.

Or we have this, in another letter to the same correspondent:

> I find the 'state of the nation' quite terrifying ... In ten years' time we shall *all* be cowering under our beds as rampaging hordes of blacks steal anything they can lay their hands on. Enoch [Powell] was right – can't see why they call him a fool.

Enough already. Certainly Larkin would not have been offered the post of Poet Laureate (which he declined) had the volume of his letters been published at the time. Nor, I presume, been made a Companion of Honour. We all know

that writers can be bad – Byronically bad – but presumably there are ill-defined lines that cannot be crossed. It's a
wonder that T. S. Eliot, and his fellow anti-Semites Virginia
Woolf and Ezra Pound, manage to stay on Professor Jardine's university's syllabus.

Fortunately, though, you can say what you like in your
journal or diary, unless you are foolish enough to allow their
unexpurgated publication, as John Fowles did, exposing
more than one wants to know about both himself and his
relationships, and manifesting a fair leavening of that anti-
Semitic feeling that pops up too frequently in members of
his generation. I don't admire that – being myself the object
of some of his pointed remarks (apparently I am 'too Jewish
for English tastes') – but I am, after all, still an admirer of
some of Fowles's novels, and continue to be devoted to Eliot,
and intermittently to Woolf and to Pound. I require them
to be artists, not good people. I am not looking for friends,
nor do I feel I have a right not to be offended, especially by
great writers, whose job it can be to transgress and to challenge our most cherished ideas and values. Once you start
burning memoirs and shredding diaries, you align yourself
with the extremists who burned copies of *The Satanic Verses*,
or of the *Koran*.

Given the explosive content of the *Letters*, what might have
been in Larkin's diaries? Were they worse? (We do *not* want
him – like Byron – to be worse: there is nothing attractive
about the extremes of the Larkinian.) Robert Conquest, a
lifetime friend of Larkin's and his partner in various stealthy
visits round the porn shops of Soho in the '50s, once told me
that the diaries consisted largely of 'wanking fantasies', and
that Western literature would have suffered no loss when

they were shredded. Indeed, Larkin confided to Conquest that, once he had stripped the diaries of anything that might be creatively useful, he intended to burn them.

I have sold the archives of a great many writers. There are often diaries, journals and personal letters included in such sales, and they always involve some degree of intimate disclosure. It is not uncommon in such cases, when the friends and relatives are still alive, for the writer or his estate to stipulate that such material cannot be made available to the public for a period of time – sometimes as long as seventy-five years.

Might this not have been done with Larkin's diaries? The problem is that such decisions are always made at the wrong time, often just before or after a death. Soon after Sylvia Plath died, Ted Hughes destroyed one of her journals, thinking that its contents would have been too raw and distressing for her children, even when they were grown up. Surely, as a generation of Plath scholars has claimed, he was wrong? The journal could have been put under embargo for a period of time. I'll bet that if Hughes had thought of this, he would have done so.

It could have happened with the Larkin diaries too. In a hundred years, who would care if they were rude about a lot of largely forgotten people, or were more or less sexually revealing? Assuming that Larkin's reputation will survive, and it just might, surely our successors would learn more about him, and us, from their continued existence?

But he didn't want us to. In writing in a diary, we partake of a secular version of the confessional, in which the writer is both penitent and priest, and absolution is delivered in the very act of honest self-revelation. 'Dear Diary', we say,

implicitly mirroring 'Dear God'. In the uncensored exposure of what I 'am like' – at the Larkinian extremes of the
splenetic and libidinal – one is at one's worst and, paradoxically, best: clear-eyed, undefended, humble.

The diaries were private. According to Anthony Thwaite,
only one person (other than Mackereth) ever sneaked a look
at them, and Larkin was understandably furious. He would
have been even more outraged and humiliated – if one can
imagine being so *post mortem* – by the public exposure of
his rancid inward musings. In destroying his diaries he was
adjusting the image of himself that would prevail.

His poem 'An Arundel Tomb' concludes with an often
cited and frequently misunderstood line: 'What will survive
of us is love.' The previous line, however, makes it clear that
there are conditions attached to this sentiment, which is
'Our almost-instinct, almost true.' It is what we strive for,
and wish, and fail to achieve. But surely it is better for a little
love to survive, however mitigated, than a lot of bitchiness
and sexual fantasy?

I am anxious about the destruction of the historical
record. We live, understand and accumulate a sense of ourselves as a culture through the preservation of the pieces of
paper that record what we truly are, and have been. But I
find it hard to regret the destruction of Larkin's diaries. Our
final view of him is probably more sympathetic – indeed,
more loving – as a consequence of their ultimate cremation.

Do the dead have rights? I have always supposed so,
though it is a difficult argument, and the law is ambiguous
on the subject: it is difficult in English law, for instance, to
libel the dead. Thus if one were, say, pursuing a vendetta
against someone, and publicly and falsely labelled their

recently deceased father a paedophile, they would have no recourse to the law. It is obvious that such a claim would be distressing and infuriating to the deceased father's friends and relatives, but it also seems to me that it does an injury and injustice to the dead man himself.

Whether he still has some notional 'self' is, of course, a complex question. But emotionally and morally the case seems clear to me. Surely the decencies accorded to the living, the respect and scrupulousness with regard to fact, ought to pertain (at the very least) to the recently deceased. Because if they are genuine, such feelings, surely they are also durable?

The New Zealand Maori, amongst many other cultures, venerate their ancestors, and it is regarded as an egregious insult to malign a person's deceased relatives. Our attitude, in contrast, assumes that, even if the deceased ascends to Heaven, they cannot be libelled there, and have passed well beyond any exposure to, or interest in, terrestrial human affairs. What they do up there has never been clear to me, but it clearly isn't worrying about their reputations.

Can we, rising direct from the death-bed, say, of Philip Larkin, happily and publicly brand him a pornography addict and lecher, a racist, a pathetic Little-Englander? There is some truth in all these charges, but not the required decency and circumspection, not the respect due to a person and to the memory of that person.

His letters reveal a misogynistic, ultra-right-wing racism that he jokily regarded as a bit of plain-speaking, but unless you were predisposed in his favour, it was merely repellent. He was not, in this respect, a very sympathetic person, though the fact that virtually everyone who knew him loved him suggests that you can get away with quite a lot, opinion-wise, if you are funny and honest and charming. And he was careful to behave properly in public.

Anyway, all that stuff about, say, masturbating over pictures of (mock) schoolgirls being spanked is pretty tame stuff, especially by today's standards – nothing to get in a huff about, is it? We all have sexual habits and fantasies that we would be chagrined to have made public. But what if Larkin's diaries revealed both fantasies *and* practices that were less (as it were) harmless? Perhaps Larkin destroyed his diaries because they were darker, more embarrassing and more compromising than one might have expected? Let's suppose that the diaries demonstrate not only a predilection for spanking, but that the recipients of the discipline were twelve-year-olds, and that Larkin often put this into practice? What would such a posthumous revelation do to our image of him, and to our readings of, and respect for, his works?

We are used to the notion that an artist does not have to be a good person to produce great art. It sometimes seems as if goodness is a positive hindrance: writers and artists, like high-class athletes, are often self-centred; they cultivate selfishness, refine and distil it. In order to get the most out of themselves, they take a lot out of others. This is no doubt hard on their friends, partners and children, but the rest of us garner the results happily enough.

Yet every now and again you learn, or come to recognise something, about an artist that is so shocking that it penetrates the way you understand them for ever more. James Joyce and Dylan Thomas were pathologically selfish scroungers? Who cares? Most authors are a bit like that. But what are we to make of the fact that the artist Eric Gill was regularly buggering his daughters when they were young teenagers? I have never been able to look at one of those silky Gill female nudes, or his soppy sets of lovers, without a shudder of remembrance. He is ruined for me.

How can one justify revaluing the work on the basis of the life? After all, if you did not know this about Gill, and I showed you his pictures, your response to them would be, as it were, purely aesthetic. Perhaps you admire them very much? And then you are told the salient facts which have put me off them: what are you to do with them? Look again at the images and recoil? And what is it you would thus be rejecting: the image or the life? They are supposed to be separable, but I have never managed to compartmentalise my responses so clearly. How morally corrupt is an artist allowed to be before we feel justified in turning our backs towards their work?

I had exactly this problem once, in my rare book business, with an illustrated manuscript, entitled *The Boy's Own Book of Spankings*, by T. H. White, the author of *The Sword in the Stone*, a writer admired by many and loved by some. The three bound volumes, clearly intended for private enjoyment, consisted of a text of some 160 pages, together with graphic photographs – clearly taken from the life – of boys with severely whipped bottoms, the stripes and abrasions and bruises lovingly recorded and amplified by the camera. Certain that the material would be of interest to biographers of White, I offered it to the Manuscripts Librarian at the British Library. She replied that she would not be interested in purchasing it, not because it was of no interest, but because it disgusted her. I argued that it was not her job to make moral judgements on the quality of material she purchased, but she wasn't to be moved.

'Yuck!' she said, and it was eventually sold to a private collector. I was never told why he was interested in them, and made sure not to ask.

Such prurient information, of course, eventually has a way of making itself into the public domain. Take the case of James Joyce, whose erotic letters to his fiancée, Nora Barnacle, sent from Trieste in 1909, are pornographic, obsessional, scatological, distinctly graphic. They were published by a (mildly reluctant) Richard Ellmann in 1975, by which time Joyce's reputation could easily enough survive their disclosure. He was enshrined, by then, in the canon. But suppose they had been published immediately after his death? Would their explicit obscenity not inevitably have leaked into a discussion of his work, thrown it, somehow, out of balance?

We are critically so obsessed by tracing life into work, uncovering and disclosing the unconscious underpinning of the creative act, that it makes revelations about the private life of the artist more important, I feel, than they actually are. Hence our fascination with the literary archives of writers, their diaries and journals, the uncensored divulgation. Artists, like the rest of us, have their little secrets. That these need mapping onto the life's work strikes me as dubious, as it would be for those of us who have similar secrets, but nothing (as it were) to show for them. I doubt very much whether my life as an academic and writer has very much to do with those aspects of my life that I am happy to keep private. Why shouldn't Philip Larkin, Lord Byron and James Joyce be afforded the same degree of kindly discretion?

8

Déjà Vu All Over Again:
The Trial in Israel

I first read Kafka's *The Metamorphosis* at the age of eighteen, in Freshman English 101 at the University of Pennsylvania. It was on the syllabus, I suppose, to serve as an introduction for naïve readers as to the nature and purposes of metaphor. The story begins abruptly enough: 'As Gregor Samsa awoke one morning from uneasy dreams he found himself transformed in his bed into a gigantic insect-like creature.' (Vladimir Nabokov suggested a beetle with wings under his shell, capable of flight, though Kafka had insisted he had no particular creature in mind.) At first, Gregor is bemused by his new incarnation, but no amount of doubt or interrogation of his physical form will make it go away. He was a person, and now he is a bug. His poor sister Grete is initially kind to him, but his parents are repulsed, and conditions, and *his* condition, deteriorate rapidly. At the end of the story he dies, wretched and abandoned, in a corner of the room.

It is a harrowing story, bleakly comic at points, and Gregor's isolation and alienation from his loved ones, his irremediable misery and loneliness, are emblems, I was informed, of the human predicament, of the absurdity of our existence. We are all Gregor Samsas, isolated in a brittle carapace, waiting alone for the inevitable end, misunderstood, incapable of communication, lacking sustenance. It's not a beetle's life, it's everyone's, only taken to this new metaphorical extreme.

I didn't believe it for a minute, the image was too far removed from the human condition to stand as an emblem of what and who we all are. You might as well suppose we are all cauliflowers, or chipmunks. I protested vehemently to our instructor. The difference between persons and beetles is too extreme, I asserted, to serve as the basis for some analogy.

'That's the purpose of metaphor,' he said smugly. 'One thing has to be understood in terms of another.'

I acceded gracelessly, and was eventually cowed – or cynical – enough to write an essay about Kafka's brilliant use of metaphor in our final exam, and got an 'A'. But I was faking it then, and re-reading the story since, I more or less agree with my younger self. Though *The Metamorphosis* certainly has some metaphoric implications, they are delicately poised, and better left uninterrogated. There is no allegory here, no parable. The power of the story lies in its literalness, it is particular and exact: it is what it is, a sort of horror story, perfectly imagined and forensically described, of what it would be like to wake up as a big bug. Did Kafka suppose himself, and all of us, to be – as it were – trapped in our own symbolic insectitude? I doubt it very much; he was far too intelligent for that. But what he did know, and could make us experience with chilling acuity, was how – given the absurd premise – it would feel to be thus metamorphosed.

Franz Kafka and his dog looking pensive.

And if the loneliness and desperation of the transformed Gregor Samsa ring some bells, so much the better.

He meant exactly what he said; he needed no interpretation. All you had to do was read him, and I loved it. Every day for the next two months I would go down to the Van Pelt Library in the late afternoon and read Kafka in entranced admiration, slouched in an upholstered chair covered in scratchy orange material, with bleached wooden arms, in the downstairs reception area. For those weeks I became one of the fixtures. I hesitated to borrow the books, which was my usual habit. Nor did I wish to own them. It felt curiously wrong to treat his books as takeaways, like literary pizza. There was something satisfying about the ritual of encountering Kafka in what was, I recognised, a space that he could have created himself: there's something chilling about the rituals and implacable procedures of a library – the organising, shelving, cataloguing, circulating – its imposed silences and grey guardians at the gates.

Reading Kafka when I was eighteen remains the only time in my reading life in which I have been unambiguously happy in a library, without anxiety or self-consciousness, unintimidated by the demands of scholarship or the need to prove myself. All I wanted was to read. Not for any purpose – it was not useful to my coursework, and I cannot recall talking to anyone about it. It was motivated by pure, untrammelled curiosity, and a cause of delight.

When I had finished the available short stories, novels, collections of letters and biographies, I felt bereft and oddly resentful to have been left with a craving for more. Yes, I acknowledged, it was astonishing that this young, rather sickly lawyer, with a full-time job in the insurance industry, could have produced so much in so little available spare time. I was hooked on Kafka, and unreasonably resentful that he had let me down by not producing more. Like Oliver Twist, forever hungry: 'Please, sir, can I have some more?' I tried reading Camus, but compared to Kafka it felt thin, and a bit formulaic.

Prior to his death in 1924, at the age of forty, Franz Kafka had published few of those great works for which he is remembered, and his passing was hardly noted. There were a number of short stories, including a slim volume containing *A Hunger Artist*, and *The Metamorphosis*, but the great novels for which he is revered had not been published for the simple reason that he did not wish them to be. He left explicit instructions to his dear friend (also a lawyer) Max Brod about what to do with the material: 'Dearest Max, my last request: Everything I leave behind me ... in the way of diaries, manuscripts, letters (my own and others'), sketches, and so on, to be burned unread.' Indeed, towards the end of his life Kafka himself burned some of the work, and we can only speculate why he left the bulk of it for Brod to dispose of, when he could have done so himself.

It was an unambiguous final request, and Brod, to his great credit, and perhaps intuiting Kafka's ambivalence about the matter, ignored it. Over the next ten years he prepared the manuscripts for publication, as *The Trial* (1925), *The Castle* (1926) and *Amerika* (1927) – probably the works for which the author is best known, and from which the adjective 'Kafkaesque' is appropriately derived – appeared in German editions (the language in which they were written).

This story is so well known – as worn by usage as are the many accounts of, say, the assassination of John F. Kennedy

– that it is almost impossible to relate the bare facts with any vivacity. Most popular accounts of Kafka sound like Wikipedia entries (as diligent and prosaic as my previous two paragraphs), while most academic writing about him strives so desperately for something original by way of interpretation or textual analysis that it is hardly of interest even to other practitioners of the Kafka trade, much less to Kafka's multitude of admiring readers. While his stories continue to provoke and to enthral, Kafka's own story, once the simple facts have been laid down, seems to have lost much of its power to surprise or to move us. Nothing much more to be said, is there?

But he has a curious haunting resonance, Franz Kafka. If he is not still with us, he has an insistent quality that makes us wish ardently that he were. His works have been made into songs, novels, films, biopics, operas, as if he were endlessly demanding to be re-understood, reanimated and reassessed. He is alive to us as few authors are, and it is no surprise that he has insinuated himself into the imagination of so many creative writers. Philip Roth wrote a marvellous piece on Kafka, which falls into two distinct parts: the first, a magisterial revisiting of the author, invoking his physical presence and imagining what might have been had he not died so young, and the second, as if imaginatively required, a fantasy in which a middle-aged refugee, Dr Kafka, shows up in Newark to teach Hebrew to the nine-year-old Roth (who cruelly refers to him as Dr Kishka) and a few of his friends at the local *schul*.

The lonely bachelor is soon invited to the Roths' table, and hesitantly begins to court Aunt Rhoda, an unprepossessing frump whom the exiled writer miraculously begins to invigorate. Next thing you know, she is about to star in the local play. It is touching, funny, with a surprising plausibility, and it ends – as it must – in tears. Though attracted, Kafka cannot commit. It is the story of his life, and it is necessary in this poignantly comic counter-life as well. He forswears Rhoda, dies once again, alone, with his piles of unpublished manuscripts unknown to his few acquaintances. We are left to assume, and to imagine, that they are thrown out with his few possessions after he dies. Even reincarnated imaginatively, he teases, disappoints and leaves us with nothing more than we had before.

Roth's effort is representative, and symbolic. But even his imaginative powers, and sympathy for both the man Kafka and for his works, cannot create what cannot be made. It is not up to Philip Roth to write more Kafkas, as, say, Kingsley Amis, John Gardner and Sebastian Faulks made more James Bonds following Ian Fleming's death. James Bond is only James Bond, thin and predictable – almost anyone could do a recognisable version of him – but you can't do more Kafka. You can parody him, or do a pastiche of the Kafka-esque, but the best of his works are so precisely individuated, so entirely his own, that it would be a ludicrous presumption to attempt more of them.

That's a fact. We have our favourite artists, composers, writers. They do their work, and they leave us. What they have not done remains undone, and if our internal and external landscapes are haunted by the unaccomplished possibilities – the lost buildings of Charles Rennie Mackintosh, the further poems of Keats or symphonies of Mozart – we simply have to do without them. Anyway, we were lucky with Kafka: had it not been for Max Brod's unwillingness to destroy the unpublished material, all we would have had was an obscure writer who published a few short stories during his lifetime.

When reading Kafka in my orange chair at Penn, I assumed – as most readers did – that Brod had chosen both discriminatingly and exhaustively when he edited Kafka's manuscripts and prepared them for publication. Either there was nothing more, or there was nothing more that was fit to print. It was a reasonable presumption, and for some seventy years there was no reason to challenge it. And when such a reason began to emerge, the details were so remarkable, so unlikely, and so fraught, that they could only have been invented by the master himself. *Kafka was back.*

Or was he? To understand the manifold complexities and ironies of this question, we have to return to 1939, when Max Brod, as the Nazis marched into Prague, departed in haste for Palestine, taking with him everything that he most valued. On arrival he was to continue his prolific career as a writer, involve himself in the theatre and settle into an apparently secure and uncontentious life. As far as one can ascertain, no one outside his immediate circle knew that he had taken with him from Prague two suitcases full of further Franz Kafka material.

What was in the suitcases? Why had he chosen not to reveal their contents? How important were the documents? Brod left no answers to these questions. What he did leave, though, was the contents of the suitcases themselves, which passed after his death in 1968 (his wife having predeceased him) to Esther Hoffe, a long-time friend, secretary and (it was widely presumed) lover. It has still not been established exactly what Brod's wishes in the matter were: whether Hoffe was to hold the papers in trust, before passing them on to an appropriate library (though why Brod would choose such an unwieldy process is unclear), or whether she simply took over ownership of the material under the terms of the will. There are numerous and contradictory accounts of what has followed since that time, mostly released through newspapers and the wire services, and which differ in crucial details.

The following timeline and narrative seem the most likely account. Esther Hoffe, in the years after acquiring the Kafka material, behaved as if she unambiguously owned it and had the sole right to determine if, how and when it should be sold. In 1974 a series of letters and postcards from Kafka to Brod were privately sold to a buyer or buyers in Germany. The fact was not unnoticed in Israel, and Hoffe was regarded as the most likely source of the material. Somebody was clearly keeping an eye on her, because when, the very next year, she attempted to board a flight from Israel to Germany, she was stopped at customs, searched and found to have a cache (no one has revealed quite what was in it) of Kafka material for which, she was told, she needed to have deposited photocopies at the National Library as a condition of export. This did not stop her – nor is it entirely clear why it should have – from selling the handwritten manuscript of Kafka's *The Trial* at Sotheby's in London, in 1988, for a price of just under $2 million, which was then the highest price ever fetched for a twentieth-century literary manuscript. It was purchased by the German Museum of Modern Literature in Marbach, which has the largest collection of Kafka manuscript material, and which has continued to claim that Max Brod wished all of his material to end up there.

Presumably that manuscript did not need a formal export licence (it may have been kept abroad), but it seemed to the Israelis that it needed at the very least a moral one. According to a spokesman for the Israeli National Library, Brod's will had apparently stipulated that the material left in Hoffe's possession was destined to be deposited there upon her death. But Hoffe's lawyers cited a 1974 judgement of an Israeli district court which ruled that Brod had gifted the collection to her, and that she had the right to give or sell it to any institution of her choice, whether in Israel or abroad.

Returning the manuscript of *The Trial* to Israel would 'correct an ongoing historic injustice', Israel National Library director Shmuel Har Noy told the newspaper *Haaretz*. The phrase is both opaque and provocative, and it was many years before the underlying assumptions and arguments were clarified and made public. It was already clear, looking at what is known of these transactions, that there was some problem with Frau Hoffe's possession of the Kafka papers, only no one would say *exactly* what it was. Nor was it clear who this 'no one' consisted of. There was no statement regarding the matter from what one can only call The Authorities, who were palpably watching her closely and assuming some wrong-doing.

It was as if *The Trial* were being re-enacted in Israel: mysterious, sinister and infuriating. In that novel, an investigating policeman makes this point to poor Joseph K. when he is first arrested: 'Our authorities, as far as I know … don't go out looking for guilt among the public; it's the guilt that draws them out, like it says in the law, and they have to send us police officers out. That's the law.'

If *The Metamorphosis* resists analysis as metaphor, *The Trial* seems to demand it, and is often regarded as Kafka's most approachable version of man's fate. Joseph K., a thirty-year-old Chief Clerk at a bank in which he is held in high esteem, leading, so far as one can see, a blameless bachelor's life, is suddenly told he is under investigation by the judiciary and police, for a crime or crimes which are never specified. This sinister procedure is not directed at him alone; it can and does happen frequently to others, who are similarly ignorant of the complaints levelled against them, and of the processes by which they will be tried, or through which they can defend themselves. A sprawling, tawdry and floppily implacable judiciary resides over this deathly shambles, and teams of lawyers and experts, of one sort or another, attempt to navigate these murky byways, and fail. Within a year Joseph K., having moved from initial bemusement and spirited resistance to a weary if uncomprehending acceptance that he cannot defend himself – no one is found innocent – is taken off in the night-time by two burly functionaries and stabbed in the heart, dying 'like a dog' in an abandoned quarry. He accepts his fate but never understands it: a process that certainly seems to have some generalisable implication.

In the meantime, Frau Hoffe continued in residence in her Jerusalem apartment with (according to most reports) some of the Kafka material – the rest apparently deposited in safe-deposit boxes in both Tel Aviv and Zurich – and her many cats. It was, by most accounts, a most insalubrious environment (unless you were a cat), and visitors, other than her daughters, were unwelcome. Scholars appealed desperately to be given access to the material and were unceremoniously dismissed. Whether The Authorities attempted to enter the premises is unrecorded, and (if they did) what the outcome was is unknown.

Esther Hoffe died, aged 101, in 2007 and left the material, still under the firm impression that she was its rightful owner, to her daughters, who themselves had no doubt that they now owned it, or about what to do with the material. It would be sold, they announced through an attorney, as if it were a bag of oranges:

> If we get an agreement, the material will be offered for sale as a single entity, in one package. It will be sold by weight ... They'll say: 'There's a kilogram of papers here, the highest bidder will be able to approach and see what's there.' The National Library [of Israel] can get in line and make an offer, too.

This bizarre and unprecedented procedure can itself indicate how little either the heirs or their lawyers understood about the importance of the material, or the proper ways of appraising its value. Indeed, even a buyer of oranges likes to inspect them before purchase. The value of such material correlates exactly to its importance: has it been published before? How significant is it biographically or in literary terms? In short: what can be learned from it? The manuscript of *The Trial* didn't weigh much, but it is one of the iconic novels of the twentieth century, and would undoubtedly have fetched many times more than a cache of lesser material which weighed twice as much. It doesn't add to one's confidence in lawyers. Unless this one was kidding – good joke! – though Israeli lawyers with a sense of humour are an endangered species.

No one outside the immediate circle of those arguing and advising on the proceedings had been informed about the contents of the boxes. If there was some problem with Hoffe's ownership of the papers – was she merely their custodian? – it was also unclear whether she had the legal right to pass them on to her daughters. The lawyer acting for the Israeli National Library was as outraged as only a lawyer can be: 'As long as Esther Hoffe was alive, she was responsible, she could say, "I am handling it" ... The late Mrs. Hoffe did not do what the late Mr. Brod asked her to do and deposit the documents in the National Library ... The will was not honoured, it was desecrated.' *The Trial*, again, is a perfect guide to the absurdity of the process: 'Needless to say, the documents would mean an almost endless amount of work. It was easy to come to the belief, not only for those of an anxious disposition, that it was impossible ever to finish it.'

But there was a much more complex question at issue, which lay in the baffling claim that the Kafka papers are essential to the Jewish heritage, and hence are the *natural* property of the state. According to David Blumberg, chairman of the board of directors of the National Library, 'The library does not intend to give up on cultural assets belonging to the Jewish people ... Because it is not a commercial institution and the items kept there are accessible to all without cost, the library will continue its efforts to gain transfer of the manuscripts that have been found.' The implications of this remarkable assertion, according to Judith Butler, who has written one of the most thoughtful pieces on the subject, are breath-taking:

The implicit understanding is that all ... Jewish cultural assets – whatever that might mean – outside Israel eventually and properly belong to Israel ... if the National Library claims the legacy of Kafka for the Jewish state, it, and institutions like it in Israel, can lay claim to practically any pre-Holocaust synagogue, artwork, manuscript or valuable ritual object extant in Europe.

It is hard to see how such an argument could convince anyone who has the slightest degree of sense, much less of justice.

Nor would Kafka himself have acceded to this easy description of himself as somehow essentially Jewish, hence naturally assimilable to the state's claim that his work was one of its cultural assets. Kafka was by temperament and inclination an outsider, his major commitment being to the inconsistent ways in which he engaged with the world. He was, he observed in a letter, 'excluded from every soul-sustaining community on account of my non-Zionist (I admire Zionism and am nauseated by it), non-practising Judaism'.

In 2009 the Tel Aviv Family Court required that the papers be examined before giving its ruling on the question of their ownership and eventual destination. This process was apparently envisaged as taking several weeks. But it took almost two years, in which the ten lawyers involved could hardly be crammed into the under-sized room in which the court met.

The room they've been allocated, with its narrow space and low ceiling, will be enough to show what contempt the court has for these people. The only light in the room comes through a little window that is so high up that, if you want to look out of it, you first have to get one of your colleagues to support you on his back.

These proceedings were so complex and protracted, the procedures so opaque, that it is impossible, once again, not to invoke Kafka's great novel.

Advocates, civil servants, experts and witnesses milled about, uncertain what the procedures were, and where each of them fitted in. Indeed, according to Reuters, 'lawyers twice asked what exactly the deliberation was all about'. *The Trial* again describes just such an absurd process:

> there are so many various opinions about the procedure that they form into a great big pile and nobody can make any sense of them. ... Even for the junior officials, the proceedings in the courtrooms are usually kept secret, so they are hardly able to see how the cases they work with proceed, court affairs appear in their range of vision often without their knowing where they come from and they move on further without learning where they go.

It was not until February 2011 that these obscure deliberations reached a point when a rough sense of the documents in the safe deposit boxes began to emerge. The wire services noted the presence of the manuscripts of 'Wedding Preparations in the Country' (previously published, but from incomplete fragments) and a few other short stories, some Kafka diaries and correspondence, and Brod's unpublished diaries. The Oxford Professor of German, Richie Robertson, noted that 'potentially the most interesting item is Max Brod's own diaries ... used for his own biography of Kafka, in which he quoted numerous passages about Kafka.' It is hard to follow his reasoning without seeing the material, but it would seem likely that the discovery of a previously unknown version of a story by Kafka is a more exciting discovery than any amount of diaries by Kafka's friend and amanuensis. Maybe it's not a very good short story? But, the professor observes, 'there may be more', and until we know exactly what this might be, it is still hard to make a judgement. It will take some further time before we can assess fully the nature and importance of what is, at long last, revealed.

On October 14, 2012, the case was (presumably) decided in an overcrowded Tel Aviv court, when it was ruled that the papers were – wait for it! – the rightful property of the state of Israel. Presumably this came as a surprise to no one except Esther Hoffe's daughters, who have announced they will appeal against the judgement.

But according to Judge Talia Kopelman-Pardo, the case was clear enough: Brod's will of 1948 did not gift tens of thousands of pages to Esther Hoffe, but instead stipulated that they should 'go to the library of the Hebrew University in Jerusalem or the Tel Aviv Municipal Library ...' (That this sentence concluded with the phrase 'or any other public institution in Israel or abroad,' would certainly have interested the archivists in Marbach or Oxford, both holders of more Kafka material than there is in Israel). But the lure of these foreign possibilities cut no ice with the judge. The papers were in Israel, and there they would stay. Unless, of course, another flurry of obscure legal activity on behalf of the sisters managed to free them.

To its credit, the Hebrew University intends to publish all the material online, once the case is finally decided and the necessary processes can be completed. That, according to Oxford's Professor Robertson, is an unambiguously good thing, though he doubts how much important primary material may be revealed. But the redoubtable English novelist Will Self was sniffy about the whole business: 'Brod himself was intent on canonising Kafka as a Zionist saint (! – sceptical exclamation mark supplied) and the Israeli state holding the papers ensures that this falsification (! – ditto) will continue apace …'

I haven't re-read Kafka for forty years. I had a second read-through when first teaching English at the University of Warwick in the 1970s, but since then have not been tempted to return. The reason for this, I suspect, is that he is a young person's writer, not in the sense that only the young can appreciate him, but because on first exposure he is so comprehensively and unexpectedly formative that you may never feel the need to read him again. He becomes part of you, and your mind and spirit and view of the human condition are inhabited by his stories, his views, and especially by his characters: by poor persecuted Josef K., by Gregor Samsa trapped in his rotting shell, by the hunger artist, yearning to find something, anything, that is actually good to eat, by poor K., who can't get into that castle to visit the Authorities. *Kafkaesque*: a world incomprehensible, alienating and threatening, absurd. We visit it with incomprehension and at our peril, lost at all points, disorientated, inoculated against faith, searchers for meaning in a book – and universe – that either has none, or in which it lurks inaccessibly. Once you have read Kafka, you know this.

So Kafka is like Keats? Keats died at the age of twenty-five, and as far as we know there is nothing left to be discovered. We had presumed that Kafka, dead at the age of forty, was in the same category. But Kafka, being Kafka, seems constantly likely to spring a surprise, to astound and to mystify. And however fascinating the new material – how can it not be? – there is a sense of loss attached to it, as well as an enormous excitement at something found. For we will have, in the next years, as the new material makes its way into the public domain, to revise our sense of Kafka, to reassess and reinvigorate him, to think again, and further.

I like thinking again, that's fine with me. But I also have my inner pantheon of writers and artists who are more or less set into place, and it unsettles me when something potentially cataclysmic happens to make me have to reassess them. This cataclysm can sometimes involve new biographical information. Who can now look at Eric Gill with the same affection and respect, after reading Fiona MacCarthy? Or Philip Larkin, with all that ugly talk of 'Reds' and 'niggers'? Or Ezra Pound, after encountering his anti-Semitic tirades and defence of Fascism? Because once such material enters the mind, it cannot be swept aside, marginalised or compartmentalised: we do not read an author *qua* author, denuded of personality and history: we read a fully fledged person, and some of these imperfect beings are more sympathetic than others.

But we are used to this, this uncertain mapping of the artist onto his work, and we are fully aware that great works of art can issue from decidedly uncongenial personalities. What seems to me more dangerous is the discovery, not of unsettling sexual or political information about an artist, but of previously unknown works which undermine our received image of him or her.

New Kafka stories? It makes me nervous. I can hardly wait to read them, unlike Will Self's next novel.

9

The Archive of the Penetralium of Mystery

It is the most famous opening line, perhaps, of any modern poem, as well as the most frequently misquoted: 'April is the cruellest month', the words with which T.S. Eliot's *The Waste Land* begins. In fact, the *complete* opening line actually reads 'April is the cruellest month, breeding', but the point I wish to make here is that – correctly or incorrectly quoted – the phrase is immediately recognisable, set in our memories as it is in literary history, immutable.

So it comes as something of a shock when we learn that Eliot never intended this as his opening line, and only settled on it after the acute editorial intervention of Ezra Pound, who recommended that Eliot abandon, entirely, the original opening section of the poem, an account of some rowdy Irishmen after a night on the town in Boston, full of drunken song and allusions to popular culture, which began: 'First we had a couple of feelers down at Tom's place.' Hardly the opening of *The Waste Land*, is it? But then again, it wasn't: at that point in the composition of the manuscript – some time in 1921 – the provisional title was *He Do the Police in Different Voices*.

Ezra Pound was so active and trenchant in editing the original typescript – largely in pruning and rearranging – that the final poem is occasionally referred to as a 'collaboration' between the two poets, though neither of them would have sanctioned the term. Eliot admitted that he 'placed before [Pound] in Paris the manuscript of a scrawling, chaotic poem', and certainly Pound did not hesitate to claim his role in its final incarnation:

If you must needs enquire
Know diligent Reader
That on each Occasion
Ezra performed the caesarean Operation.

But if Pound was the midwife–surgeon, what was born was pure Eliot: it was Ezra's role simply to help him to deliver the best that was in him.

This fascinating information has been available since 1971, when Eliot's widow, Valerie, published an annotated scholarly edition of the original typescript of the poem, entitled *The Waste Land: A Facsimile and Transcript of the Original Drafts Including the Annotations of Ezra Pound,* which reproduced the emendations and comments not merely of Pound but also of Eliot's first wife, Vivien. Study of this text teaches one not merely about *The Waste Land* and about Eliot and Pound, but also about how great poetry generally comes to be and how it works. It reminds us that a poem can undergo repeated processes of composition, consideration and revision, until the final form of the work has been decided upon, and published.

We know all of this because the corrected and annotated

The home of many a fine isolated verisimilitude.

typescript of *The Waste Land* can be found in the Berg Collection of the New York Public Library, which acquired it in 1968. It had originally been purchased directly from Eliot, following its publication in 1922, by the great patron of modernism the New York lawyer and collector John Quinn, and was widely assumed to have been lost, since it did not appear in the five-volume sale of Quinn's books and manuscripts held at the Anderson Gallery in 1923–4 (at which a holograph manuscript of James Joyce's *Ulysses* was sold for $5,000). But it had, in fact, been hibernating amongst Quinn's papers since his death in 1924.

The Berg Collection is a fitting final home for the manuscript because it contains the papers and manuscripts of many great writers – Auden, Conrad, Dickens, Hardy, Woolf, Yeats – and is certainly one of the repositories of literary archives that students and scholars are most likely to visit when doing their research. A few years after their acquisition of the Eliot manuscript, I went to Berg myself to study some Conrad material while doing my D.Phil. at Oxford, though the highlight of my time there was not the (terrific) Conrad material, but the hour or two that I spent with Eliot's typescript. I did not know then that my final engagement with literary manuscripts and archives would be as a dealer rather than a scholar, but the magic of literary manuscripts, as both scholarly objects and cultural treasures, was finger-tinglingly obvious. Since that time literary archives have been central to my life, and have provided occasional sources of epiphany, but also a lot of drudgery, sorting out the occasional wheat from the manifold chaff. What one encounters in the vitrines of libraries is the result of the sifting of voluminous amounts of material.

I once attended a conference on literary archives at the home of so many of them, the Harry Ransom Center at the University of Texas at Austin. The conference stretched – interminably to me, for I am impatient and not very good at such things – over three days, and covered more topics about archives than most people would wish to know. What is the future of literary archives? How will they be affected by changes in digital technology? What new ways have been devised for information recording and retrieval?

Yawn, alas. Alas, because I make part of my living dealing in literary archives, so I ought to have been interested in such questions, and intermittently I was. Did you know that a techno-wizard can retrieve *every* keystroke made on a keyboard and recorded on a hard disc? This means not only will you be found out having watched (and deleted) *Swedish Nurses 37*, but all of the emendations, alterations, changes and corrections of an author's literary compositions can be located, recovered and eventually made available for hyperdiligent perusal.

But though I spend a lot of my time with archives, this does not mean that I unalloyedly enjoy it, or them. Let's start at the beginning. An archive consists of the mass of personal papers that fill a writer's study, and attic, and (if you ask their partner) most of the rest of the house. The terminal moraine of an author's life. What is to be found there? Well, in ideal state – with, as Gertrude Stein put it, 'no pieces of paper thrown away' – you might find: the author's manuscripts and drafts of work both published and unpublished; diaries or journals; incoming correspondence and (if you are very lucky) copies of the author's outgoing letters as well; historical material that documents the author's life, photographs and family memorabilia; objects of significance: the writer's desk, typewriter or computer, or (even) best Sunday suit. This material will have spread like an infestation through the house, and found nesting places in boxes and cartons, filing cabinets, bookshelves and drawers both open and secret ('no one is looking into my drawers!' William Golding once warned me, a little ambiguously).

When first encountered, an archive reminds me of a monkfish. When it is eventually served up to you in bite-sized morsels, accompanied by rice and a salad, it is enticing enough, but when you see it in an unfilleted state it is ugly, cumbersome and presumably unpalatable. I have spent a lot of time in attics, studies and cellars, sifting through myriad unsorted boxes and cartons of a writer's stuff – dust! damp! – and there is something lowering about the process, something dirty and invasive that makes you both literally and figuratively need a wash.

When, eventually, you have carted it away and sold it to an institution which has catalogued it assiduously, and then put it on display or exhibition, an archive bursts into life. It is, after all, on the basis of such collections of assiduously preserved pieces of paper that we come to have accurate recordings of ourselves and others: biographies get written, journals are published, Collected Works and Letters are published, history is *made*.

This will seem, on the face of it, an unambiguously good thing. We are wedded, in this archival world, to documenting the *development* of texts: how does a literary work begin, what stages does it go through before it reaches its final form? This produces fascinating results, like the one with which I began this chapter. Yet it occurs to me that this process, of tracing things through their stages, as if they were persons growing up, may have the concomitant danger of over-emphasising the importance of process at the expense of product.

Of course, we are fascinated, whether as parents or gardeners, by watching things grow and develop. I recently had the privilege of reading carefully through Geoffrey Hill's many working notebooks of poetry, and it was riveting to watch the poems develop, contract, wind back upon themselves, searching for their final form of words. That is exciting, but such knowledge is purchased at some cost, isn't it? The special status of the final form of the text is mitigated. When we do not have any indication of the writing process – as we do not with, say, Shakespeare – the received texts have an *inevitability* about them, as if they could hardly be other than they are. And this apparent un-negotiability enforces their otherness and suggests some mystery in their composition, as if it were impossible that they could be other than they are. I am glad there is no Shakespeare archive. I'm delighted not to know what the other Commandments might have been, when God originally drafted them. Show me a few rejected drafts – *Thou Shalt Only Eat Kosher Food* – and the power and authority of the Ten will diminish. It could have been otherwise, could it? Why obey then? Maybe they will change again?

Remember that great phrase of Keats, describing how Coleridge 'would let go by a fine isolated verisimilitude caught from the Penetralium of mystery, from being incapable of remaining content with half-knowledge'? By way of contrast, Keats instances Shakespeare, who, possessed of 'Negative Capability', was content to allow 'uncertainties, mysteries and doubts' without attempting to resolve or rationalise them. I cite this because I believe we strip something numinous from our texts, reduce and denature them, when we focus too intently on *how they came to be*, and too little on the fact that *they are*. As if the purpose of literary research was to produce Variorum Editions, which exhaustively collate all known versions and variants of the text. I'm glad there is no archive of the Penetralium of Mystery.

Our fascination with an author's manuscripts, and the development of his texts, is a relatively recent phenomenon, which, though it begins in the nineteenth century, has accelerated into orthodoxy only in the last fifty years. To a pre-twentieth-century sensibility or, indeed, in many countries of the world to this day an author's manuscripts are regarded as of little interest, because all that really matters is what the writer finally chooses to publish.

The film *Shakespeare in Love* (1998) makes the point adroitly, as well it might, for the screenplay was co-authored by Tom Stoppard, himself a sophisticated book collector. In one scene Shakespeare is seen in the process of composition and, finishing a sheet, wonders aloud whether he should keep it. 'Who'd care about that?' he is asked, and he shrugs his shoulders, and tosses it in the bin.

Well, a vast number of people would, that's for sure. The Shakespeare archive! Whatever my misgivings, however much one wants to protect the inevitability of the received text, what fascination there would surely be in visiting the corrections, drafts and revisions of *Hamlet*.

You'd learn enormously from such material, but the problem is that you can only learn it once, though you might then discuss it in academic journals *ad nauseam*. Having discovered 'First we had a couple of feelers at Tom's place', you cannot rediscover it, only colonise and inhabit it, and in so doing ironically diminish it. It is one of those facts that startles at first, then fades into usage. So even with the best manuscript archives of the best writers there is only a limited range and potential scholarly value of such variant manuscript material. Thus when librarians and archivists consider the purchase of a writer's archive, the recurring question is 'how many books or PhDs can we get out of this?' And with corrected manuscripts, even one as important as that of *The Waste Land,* the answer is: very few.

This is even true when a manuscript is an unpublished, or perhaps incomplete work, something that never saw the light of day during an author's lifetime. William Golding's archive, for instance, contains three unpublished novels that precede *Lord of The Flies* (1955), which is on the record as his 'first' novel. Golding had tried to find a publisher for them, but after the great success of *Lord of the Flies* abandoned not the hope but the desire to find a publisher for *Seahorse, Circle under the Sea* and *Short Measure,* having come to regard them as apprentice work. It will be interesting to see if his literary executors allow their publication. If their author regarded them as inferior, might it not be interesting, nonetheless, to see him in the act of interrogating his early talent, seeking the voice and the kind of narrative that would most suit him?

Before his death in 1977, Vladimir Nabokov left instructions that an incomplete manuscript on which he had been working (later entitled *The Original of Laura*) should be destroyed. The manuscript, written on a series of 138 index (3 × 5 in.) cards, the equivalent of perhaps thirty pages of typescript, remained in the possession of the author's wife, Vera, and following her death was owned by their son Dmitri. In 2008, after three decades of consideration, he announced that the book was going to be published in the following year, and though there was much fanfare surrounding the publication, the reviews confirmed what Nabokov *père* had said in the first place: not good enough, or at least not ready for publication. Who knows what might have happened if it had been completed, revised and rewritten to Nabokov's stringent standards? Unlike Golding's unpublished early novels, which may help us to trace his early development, *The Original of Laura* allows us only an unhappy glance at a writer's apparent decline.

It would have been enough, surely, to cause Nabokov posthumously to regret not having destroyed it himself, and in this case he was less well served than Philip Larkin was by his literary executors. Or perhaps not. There is always that counter-example of Max Brod, preserving and arranging the publication of most of Kafka's life's work. But those are works of genius – you didn't need to be Max Brod to see that – whereas *The Original of Laura* is slight, incomplete and unpromising. Its publication would have distressed the fastidious Nabokov.

It is no wonder, then, that one encounters the occasional author who tries to ensure that nothing they have written survives unless they regard it as of significant quality. Jeanette Winterson once told me that she throws away manuscript drafts, corrected work, and abandoned projects, on the grounds that 'if I have decided they are not good enough for publication, why should I allow them to be seen?' She makes this point forcibly in her memoir *Why Be Happy When*

You Could Be Normal?: 'I burn my work in progress and I burn my diaries, and I destroy letters. I don't want to sell my working papers to Texas and I don't want my personal papers becoming doctoral theses.'

To Winterson, such material is not only personal, it is no longer alive, and the impulse to keep it is as absurd as the way in which Orthodox Jews preserve hair and fingernail clippings. There is not going to be a Winterson archive, and one wonders, quite, why more authors don't take this view. Perhaps there is something self-mutilating about throwing away material that might just, somehow or other, turn out to be useful. Or at least, valuable.

The major usefulness of a writer's archive, both scholarly and financial, rarely resides in manuscript material, for an author's journals and incoming correspondence often carry more scholarly potential. This can be damaging to an author's *amour propre*, when what they may (wrongly) regard as their life's work – the manuscripts – is regarded as unimportant compared with having known and corresponded with people, especially writers, more highly regarded than themselves. The archive of Al Alvarez, a central figure in the English literary scene for many decades, was of considerable value largely because he had significant relations with both Sylvia Plath and Robert Lowell, and had kept their letters. (When you are a dealer in such material, it is best *not* to make such an observation, and to gush a little about the archive 'as a whole', hoping that the owner will not decide, at the last minute, to retain the significant incoming letters and ask you to sell the rest.)

The impulse to do so is not uncommon. It is one thing to sell your own manuscripts and journals, quite another to sell

letters written to you, most often on the reasonable assumption that they were private. Though there comes a point
when an author is sufficiently well known to be aware that his
or her letters may be collected one day – and hence becomes
that little bit less forthcoming – in the early moments of a
literary career unguarded transmission of personal material
is frequent, and frequently (later) embarrassing. Letters are
supposed to be private, aren't they?

Some time in the 1980s I visited the elderly Brian Coffey,
now a rather neglected Irish writer, poet and philosopher,
hoping to place his papers with an appropriate institution. The National Library of Ireland, perhaps? I was not
unaware that he had for some years in the 1920s been a
close friend of Samuel Beckett, though I did not inquire
about this until I had examined, and appreciated, Coffey's
own manuscript material.

'You were a friend of Beckett's, weren't you?' I eventually
asked over a beer and a sandwich, as we took a break from
searching through old filing cabinets and placing various
folders on a table in the kitchen.

'Oh yes, before Sam went to Paris I used to see him all the
time. We used to play golf together.'

Golf? I had been aware that Beckett had played cricket for
Trinity College Dublin – he is one of very few writers (John
Fowles is another) whose records, modest though they may
be, are enshrined in Wisden, whose obituary of the writer
notes that he

had two first-class games for Dublin University against
Northamptonshire in 1925 and 1926, scoring 35 runs in
his four innings and conceding 64 runs without taking

a wicket. A left-hand opening batsman, possessing what he himself called a gritty defence, and a useful left-arm medium-pace bowler, he had enjoyed a distinguished all-round sporting as well as academic record at Portora Royal School, near Enniskillen, and maintained his interest in games while at Trinity College, Dublin.

No mention of golf though.

'Was he any good?'

'Oh, he hit a nice ball did Sam.'

'What was his handicap?'

Coffey paused for a moment, in what I presumed was an effort to remember, but he was simply baffled by my question.

'I don't know, we never kept score, we just hit our shots and walked and had a good talk.'

You can almost imagine it as a scene from a Beckett play. Vladimir and Estragon waiting impatiently at the first tee.

'After Sam left,' I asked, 'did you keep in touch?'

'Oh yes, we wrote to each other all the time, most days.'

The correspondence is unknown, and I could think of no references to it. A cache of letters from Beckett, written on first going to Paris, at the time of his first publications and initial relationship with Joyce and the expatriate cultural milieu, would be utterly fascinating. And valuable.

'That's interesting. How many letters would you say you had from Sam?'

'Never counted. Thousands probably.'

Thousands! My mind went back to those filing cabinets. Nothing there. Perhaps one of the drawers in the dresser in the corner? Or might they have been put into a bank?

'Where do you keep them?'

'Sam's letters? Oh, I threw them away.'

Threw them away!

'Why did you do that?'

'At first, I just answered a letter, then chucked it in the bin. As you do. But after a few years, and Sam got well known, then I made sure to throw them away ...'

'Because?'

'... because they were *private*.'

By this Coffey did not mean intimate, or particularly revealing, just that they were addressed only to him. He seemed surprised, perhaps slightly bemused, that I should regard this – one look at my face would have revealed it – as regrettable.

'They were just between us,' he added.

In that period Beckett wrote proper letters of some length, full of thinking and reflecting about his new life abroad, the people he had met and the work he was contemplating. In later years, when he became famous and there were more demands on his time, he took to writing short postcards in his spidery hand, terse, exact and exacting. The sort of cards that could easily be published, which gave nothing away, if anyone were foolish enough to collect and publish them all.

But 'thousands' of early letters? Even if 'thousands' is some sort of trope here, and can be taken to mean LOADS, the gap they leave is substantial, and I have little doubt that our picture of this period in Beckett's life would be enlarged and illuminated if they had survived. And yet I have, still, great admiration for Coffey's position. It wasn't so much a matter of principle for him – he took no pride in it, and felt no need to adumbrate or to defend his thinking – it was simply, for him, a matter of consideration, of discretion, of protecting something essentially private between himself and his friend. That his friend was to become not Sam the golfer but Samuel Beckett the great writer strengthened his resolve, when for many less considerate or more venal recipients the opposite might be true. But Coffey, had he even considered a potential financial windfall, would not have been moved by it: the letters were gone, deposited in the waste paper basket one by one as they were answered. That was the right place for them.

It's a wonderful, uncompromising attitude, and when I am not bemoaning the loss to literary history, I admire it very much.

These days, however, most writers are positively anxious, at some point, to sell their archives, and the letters of their friends. But there are several impediments to a happy conclusion to this process. First, and most poignantly, most writers value their own papers, and have reason to believe that others will do so too. They are wrong. It is only a tiny percentage of authors whose archives are purchased by institutions, while the (envious) others eventually either have to throw theirs out or impose them posthumously on bemused and irritated next of kin, who don't know what to do with them either. The only thing that can be said in favour of this is that it is better than inheriting the unwieldy and unhangable contents of an unsaleable painter's studio.

Why are so few archives saleable? The reason is that so few writers merit academic research, their manuscripts, diaries and letters of insufficient interest to spark off PhD students, biographers or anyone wishing to write a book about them. It doesn't matter how popular the writer is: I do not believe the archive of Dan Brown or James Patterson would elicit any interest from university rare book and manuscript departments. Insufficient literary merit. But – there is always some sort of 'but' lurking when you talk about archives – the James Patterson archive would be of interest if he knew (and corresponded with) the right people. Suppose he had received dozens of letters, let us say, from Cormac McCarthy? Or Barack Obama?

But I suspect that this archive business is slowly drawing to an e-close. Manuscripts? Hardly anyone writes by hand any more, and those that do are over forty. Letters? Precious few, and more precious the fewer they become. Now we have emails and texts. And what library, one wonders, would wish to collect – if one knew how to do so – the tweets and texts of Salman Rushdie (who is said to fire them off in large numbers)?

This shift away from the written to the electronic word is already causing massive uncertainty in the archive world. While there is no question that the outgoing and incoming emails from an author's computer(s) can be harvested, and perhaps printed out for cataloguing, and that these will be of substantial scholarly value, it is not clear what their monetary value should be. In general, the archival world values material – in both senses of the term – that is unique. But emails could be printed out once or a hundred times. They may offer us invaluable information about a writer's interests, relationships and work habits, but no one in the rare book world has yet come up with a formula that sets a price on them. Perhaps the old standby – what the market will bear – is all we have to go on. But as individual transactions become public knowledge, there will eventually be a sort of case law that takes over: writer X's emails were valued at $10,000, so (inferior, or less collected) writer Y's emails cannot be worth as much.

But the problem is more troubling even than this because emails, with rare exception, are not as interesting as letters. Writers take time – or took time – when writing a letter, because writing was what they did, diligently and well. So the letters, say, of Lord Byron or of Philip Larkin are frequently of enormous interest in themselves: lengthy, personal, considered (or, better yet, unconsidered), they are testimony to the writer's inner life.

Emails, by way of contrast, are quick-fire missives generally intended to initiate a question or to respond to one. They are short, pedestrian, generally unconsidered flashes in the ether. We clear the contents of our Inbox as quickly and efficiently as possible, and press Delete; the contents of our post box, on the other hand, may well be cherished, read and reread, and frequently filed away.

And as for texts? U got to b kdng. Quick-fire serial rubbish by addicted teenagers, or messages telling our partners that we will be late for supper. Not merely not *literary* language, hardly language at all. Curiously, though, email compression and text-speak are foreshadowed in the letters of Ezra Pound, who developed an idiosyncratic epistolary style, with truncated syntax, compressed spelling and slangy tones that would do a literate Valley girl (an oxymoron indeed) proud. Here he is, writing from Rapallo in the early 1930s:

New man on lit/ page/ section called 'Bear Garden' open to free (not to say prophane and viorlent diskussin ...

you cd. notify people of yr/ continued existence via that medium. Or the son and heir might practice on 'em. Grey, the edtr., is trying to stir up discussion and in gen. improve the level of same.

Such Pound letters often trade on the rare book market at surprisingly modest prices. (We once sold a series of 430 of them at an overall price of £60 each, though they get a lot pricier if you buy them in ones.)

Emails and texts haven't yet found their place in the market, but electronic archives do have one advantage over paper ones: you don't get dirty and dusty collecting them, which ironically makes me think more fondly of all those sweaty times in attics, trawling about for the real things.

10

Death by Water: The Great Omar

Here's something of a poser: can you guess what the following object was? It was adorned with over 1,000 jewels and precious stones, including rubies, turquoises, amethysts, topazes, olivines, garnets and an emerald, each in its own gold setting, held together by almost 5,000 leather inlays, and 100 square feet of gold leaf was used in its production. Was it:

1. Cleopatra's girdle?
2. King Midas's tablecloth?
3. The saddle of King Arthur's horse?
4. A bookbinding executed in 1911?

You will, naturally, have guessed number 4, as being the most preposterous. A thousand precious stones? Who would be mad enough to attempt such a thing? Aside from the question of how you could stuff all those ingredients onto its covers, what book could possibly *deserve* such ornate presentation, making us imagine some moustachioed Oriental potentate luxuriating as he reads in a garden of earthly delights?

A Book of Verses underneath the Bough,
A Jug of Wine, a Loaf of Bread – and Thou
Beside me singing …

That's it: *The Rubaiyat of Omar Khayyam*, the twelfth-century Persian masterpiece, with its compelling insistence that our pleasures and rewards, if we are to have them, must be sought in this life, not the next.

Ruba'i are poems which consist of four lines, of which all but the third rhyme. These short verses are particularly well suited to the presentation of memorable images and homilies, of which Khayyam was the great master. His poems were immediately recognised as a dangerous and thrilling counsel of temptation. The work was vilified by the religious authorities as a 'tissue of error like poisonous snakes', and their author forced to make a pilgrimage to Mecca, where he prudently resolved 'to draw in the reins of his tongue and pen', lest both be forcibly removed.

Omar Khayyam (or to give him his full name, Ghiyath al-Din Abu'l-Fath 'Umar ibn Ibrahim Al-Nishapuri al-Khayyami) was the Leonardo da Vinci of the ancient Persian world, a polymath who, in a time when it was still possible, knew more or less all there was to know. He made significant contributions in the fields of philosophy and theology, mathematics, astronomy and climatology, music and, particularly, poetry. But he came to conclude, as many men of great learning have, that no amount of understanding of such abstruse matters is likely to lead to an ultimate understanding of the nature of life. We are here, for our tiny speck of time, and then gone.

'The pride of the peacock is the glory of God': the front panel of
Sangorski's Great Omar.

Myself when young did eagerly frequent
Doctor and Saint, and heard great Argument
About it and about: but evermore
Came out by the same Door as in I went.

If oblivion may be inescapable, there is much to celebrate
and to enjoy in our brief sojourn. But Omar Khayyam is
often misrepresented as a mere celebrant of the pleasures
of the flesh, a misconception promoted by his first translator
into English, Edward Fitzgerald, but shared by many clerics
in his own, and later, times. In fact, he wrote several treatises
on religious matters which, though they deny divine intervention in daily human life, or the possibility of an afterlife,
yet cannot be described as irreligious. He declared himself
a Sufi, and though his God is distant from human affairs,
that may be all to the good, allowing us to enjoy ourselves
while we can.

But it is as a poet that Omar Khayyam is remembered.
His ruba'i are not intended to be read in any given order,
and most are versions – many of which have entered into
everyday language – of the eat, drink (a lot) and be merry
school of thought. It is, ironically, a *sobering* message: there
is no ultimate reward, nothing to look forward to but dust.
Loss, all is loss. No wonder many clerics reviled him, whatever his pretensions to orthodoxy.

Yet his work has inspired readers for eight centuries, been
translated into dozens of languages and, by the turn of the
twentieth century, was a publishing sensation. There was
hardly a poet alive who could not quote from his verses.
If any book deserved an extravagant binding, this was it,
and it was given its ultimate incarnation not by the fabled

craftsmen of the East but by two Englishmen, Francis San-gorski and George Sutcliffe.

The two first met in 1896 as young men, taking an evening course in bookbinding at the Central School of Arts and Crafts in London. Their exceptional ability was soon recognised, and both were given scholarships of £20 a year for three years, to pursue their studies. Within a year they were teaching at Camberwell College of Art, and in 1901 set up premises in Bloomsbury Square as the Sangorski and Sutcliffe Bindery. During the eleven years of their ensuing partnership, the pair became the finest bookbinders in the world, moving several times to larger premises and receiv-ing commissions of the most important kind.

It was the greatest period of English bookbinding (the rival firm of Zaehnsdorf employed 180 craftsmen), and the highly elaborate bindings that Sangorski and Sutcliffe were to produce triumphantly bridged the gap between art and craft. John Stonehouse, an employee at Henry Sotheran's Bookshop in Piccadilly, offered frequent commissions to the Bindery, and declared that their binding of John Addington Symonds's *Wine, Women and Song* (a most Omar-ish title), with its depictions of grapes made from amethysts set in gold, was the most superb ever executed. It sold quickly, and gave Stonehouse a remarkable idea, which was to come to fruition some years later.

Sangorski had a taste for the mysticism of the East – his dreams, Stonehouse observed, 'must have been of Ori-ental lands and colours which he had never seen', except perhaps in the then popular musical *Kismet*, which played at the Garrick Theatre and which Sangorski saw multiple times. He loved, too, Edward Fitzgerald's translation of

The Rubaiyat, which had been published in its first English edition of 250 copies by the bookseller Bernard Quaritch in 1859.

The eccentric Fitzgerald was an unlikely bedfellow for Omar Khayyam. Hardly an unrestrained sensualist, his marriage had lasted only a few months, after which he had a few 'friendships' with men. A vegetarian who hated vegetables, he lived largely on tea, fruit, and bread and butter – a bit like Lord Byron, except for the butter – and wasn't all that keen on his jug of wine. There is a feeling of wish-fulfilment about his translation of Khayyam, for Fitzgerald had altogether too few rosebuds to gather. Indeed, Khayyam's verse could have been aimed at him, as if begging his translator to change his ways, and get more fun out of life:

> Waste not your flour, nor in vain pursuit
> Of this and that endeavour and dispute;
> Better be merry with the fruitful grape
> Than sadden after none or bitter fruit.

A studious and retiring man, Fitzgerald indulged himself immoderately only in his Oriental fantasies, though his 'rather free' (equals 'not very accurate') translation of *The Rubaiyat* was an immediate and resounding failure. So few copies sold that within two years Mr Quaritch placed the book on a stand outside his doors, offering copies at a penny apiece. (They now fetch £20,000.) A friend bought Dante Gabriel Rossetti this cut-price present, and the delighted recipient shared his new enthusiasm with Swinburne and William Morris. Further copies were purchased and exchanged, enthusiasm blossomed, and the book slowly became a word-of-mouth sensation. Over the next decades it was reviewed frequently and reprinted numerous times.

In 1884 the book was illustrated by the celebrated American artist Elihu Vedder. *The Rubaiyat* is one of Vedder's best-known works, and the complete suite of his fifty-four drawings for it was exhibited at the Smithsonian American Art Museum in 1998. Trained in Paris well before it was fashionable, Vedder learned the requisite academic skills and became known for his classical female nudes. His *Omar Khayyam* (for which he also designed the linings, cover and lettering) was notable for what the artist called a 'cosmic swirl', which he defined as the 'gradual concentration of elements that combined to form life; the sudden pause through the reverse of the movement which marks the instant of life; & then the gradual, ever-widening dispersion again of those elements into space'. The book was published in Boston by Houghton Mifflin in two formats: a fancy one on large paper, limited to 100 copies bound in leather, at $100; and a more modest, smaller copy at $25. Both sold out in six days, and set the standard for American illustrated books for many years to come. Copies of the de luxe edition now sell for as much as £25,000.

It was a happy relationship between Omar, his translator Edward Fitzgerald and Vedder himself, who commented: 'certainly three kindred spirits have here encountered each other, and although the first two missed each other on earth by eight centuries, and the last two by twelve months, still in the heart of the survivor lingers the hope that in the life "sans end" they may all yet meet.'

Vedder's celebrated edition (which now feels as clunky and dated as his contemporary Gustave Doré's similarly

outsize and lifeless illustrations) recommended itself immediately to Francis Sangorski – a fourth party in this happy
set of conjunctions of poet, translator, artist and binder. It
was *big* enough (some 15½ inches tall) and, to his eye, positively crying out for those thousand jewels. He would wave
his finger in the air, tracing possible designs if he were to
be given a commission to bind such a book: 'I would stand
three peacocks in the middle, and surround them with jewelled decoration such as has never been dreamed of before.'

In the early years of his partnership with Sutcliffe, Sangorski had already designed a number of fanciful and stun-
ningly accomplished bindings for *The Rubaiyat*, which had
so impressed Sotheran's John Stonehouse that in 1909,
after listening once again to Sangorski's description of what
he could do if only he were allowed, he offered what the
current manager of Sangorski and Sutcliffe, Rob Shepherd,
has described as 'the most incredible commission ever given
to a bookbinder in the history of the craft':

> Do it and do it well; there is no limit, put what you like
> into the binding, charge what you like for it; the greater
> the price the more I shall be pleased; provided only that
> it is understood, that what you do, and what you charge
> for, will be justified by the result; and the book when it is
> finished is to be the greatest modern binding in the world;
> these are the only instructions.

Stonehouse offered this extraordinary brief without informing his employer, who would have found it an unacceptable
risk, but felt he was justified because 'there has never been, in
the history of the Binding Trade, a man such as Sangorski'.

Jewelled bindings, which occupied a special place in San-gorski's imagination, have a thousand-year history, and appear in opulent splendour throughout the royal libraries of Europe. Yet curiously little has been written about them. I can locate no book on the subject, and even Wikipedia's tentacles stretch to only a cursory entry. When asked why this might be, Rob Shepherd could offer no explanation, though he is intending to fill the gap with a monograph on the subject.

I wonder, though, if the subject of jewelled bindings has been largely ignored, despite a plethora of information about fine bindings generally, because it is regarded as an eccentric and faintly embarrassing byway of the craft. Most fine binders would never attempt such a thing, not merely because they have not the requisite skills, but also because they regard the results at showy and excessive, and the likely buyers of such costly trinkets as equally objectionable. Certainly there is now little taste for the form. The examples one comes across at book fairs and auctions (so someone must collect them) are at least eighty years old. Jewelled bindings are now widely regarded not as art (too vulgar) but as elaborate craft, gone wrong. Describing such bind-ings, terms such as 'opulent,' 'extravagant' and 'luxurious' recommend themselves so insistently – one thumbs through the thesaurus seeking alternatives – that it feels like search-ing for adequate adjectives to describe Liberace's hair.

Sangorski once executed a jewelled binding for a *Poems* of Keats, the cover of which had vines of jewelled grapes, which may contain a fleeting allusion to the line in 'Ode to a Night-ingale' – 'With beaded bubbles winking at the brim' – but the connection is fanciful and basically meaningless. Most such bindings are conventionally described not in terms of their relationship to the texts that they cover but as jewellery: containing so many rubies, amethysts, garnets, turquoises, as if they were taken from Elizabeth Taylor's dressing table and she was going to wear them to a bibliophile's ball.

It is the number and richness of the ornamentation that seems to matter. Thus, when the newspapers picked up the story, all of a sudden the binding had 1,500 jewels. That made it even more important! But Sangorski's work had distinguished itself not merely in the amount and weight of its jewels and gold but also because, for once, it was genuinely *appropriate*. He was not merely trying to create a surface of the most extraordinary opulence, but had thought hard about the contents of the *Rubaiyat*, and was attempting to render an image of them that was both intellectually and aesthetically satisfying.

Work began on the *Rubaiyat* in 1909. Sangorski spent eight months making six different designs for the binding, with such meticulousness that he even spent a day at London Zoo watching a snake's jaws opening as it devoured a live rat. The image of a skull (on the rear cover) is so anatomically correct as to suggest substantial prior study. (Damien Hirst's *For the Love of God,* another jewel- encrusted human skull, is a similar combination of the absurd and the exquisite, and even more expensive.)

The *Omar* took over two years of full-time work – some 2,500 hours – to produce. Its front board was of unparalleled magnificence in modern binding: three peacocks – as Sangorski had always imagined them – placed at the centre beneath a Persian arch, were modelled in blue leather, their tail feathers set with topazes, their crests decorated with eighteen turquoises, their eyes with rubies. This was bordered by elaborately swirling acanthus leaves and bunches of grapes elaborately tooled with gold.

But the delights of this front image, its colourful optimism and luxury, are only part of the overall design. Fitzgerald had described the *Rubaiyat* as 'a strange farrago of the grave and the gay', as any 'gather ye rosebuds' text must be. And so the back panel contains a perfect, eerie image of a skull, executed in white calf with ivory teeth, with poppy flowers (frequently associated with death) sprouting from its eye sockets.

In 1911 Sotheran's issued a catalogue offering the book for sale at a price of £1,000. (By way of comparison, D. H. Lawrence was then teaching in Croydon at a salary of £95 a year, and the Sotheran price, if correlated to pounds sterling in 2013 would be £330,000.) A contemporary review of Sangorski's expensive masterpiece in the *Graphic* magazine confirmed that Stonehouse's commission had been triumphantly fulfilled: the binding was 'unquestionably the most magnificent production of its kind in modern times'.

The New York rare book dealer Gabriel Weiss (or Wells, as he was sometimes called) rushed to Sotheran's to see it and made an offer of £800, but was offered no more than the customary dealer's discount of 10 per cent and walked away. The book remained on display in the shop, more admired than purchased. It was then shipped to America in the hope of attracting a buyer (three-quarters of Sangorski and Sutcliffe's bindings were bought by American collectors), but because Vedder's edition did not bear the date of its publication in 1884 (which would have made it duty-free), customs officials argued that there was no proof that it was more than twenty years old, and demanded substantial duty. It was an easy enough problem to solve – all you had to produce was a letter from the publisher – but Mr Sotheran gave a peremptory order for it to be sent home immediately.

Sensibly enough, the increasingly anxious Stonehouse got back in touch with Mr Weiss to see if he might be willing to pay £750, but instead received the tough counter-offer of £650. At which point Mr Sotheran, who had never approved of the project (once he had heard of it), sent the book off in a huff to Sotheby's, to be offered for sale with no reserve price. It was a foolish time to do so: a coal strike was badly affecting the economy, and money was tight. On 29 March 1912 Weiss bought the book in the saleroom at the modest price of £405, just over half of what he had originally offered. The book, now widely known as the 'Great Omar', was packed in an oak casket to protect it from damage, ready to be shipped to its new owner in New York, who must have thought he was a pretty smart cookie. (He was: he later became the owner of Sotheran's Bookshop itself.)

To understand what happened next, you have to invoke chaos theory, and the fluttering of that butterfly's wings. On the same day that the Great Omar sold at auction, which merited some small mention in the press, a much more newsworthy event was happening in Antarctica, where Scott and his team had failed to beat the Norwegian Amundsen to the South Pole. They had been delayed, in Scott's words, 'by severe weather which does not seem to have any satisfactory cause', which had not merely retarded their progress but also led to the deaths of all of the members of the expedition on that fateful day.

According to some modern climatologists, there was a

link between the unusual conditions at the South Pole and those pertaining at the same time at the North Pole, which had experienced unseasonably warm weather – both poles affected, though in opposite ways, by La Niña warming, which saw more icebergs carved off the west coast of Greenland than in the previous fifty years.

The Great Omar was booked for its American crossing on 6 April, but due to the coal strike no further freight was taken on board. The book thus left Southampton on the next available ship, four days later. The carrier was the SS *Titanic*, and it was not long before the weather conditions that had claimed Scott's life had sunk that ship, and killed 1,517 of its passengers. On board, amongst the richly bejewelled first-class passengers, there was also a haul of over $200 million worth of diamonds, shipped by two brothers from Switzerland, as well as the 1,051 precious stones adorning Francis Sangorski's masterpiece.

Labelled 'unsinkable' by the Vice-President of the White Star Line, the *Titanic* was both the largest and the most luxurious (if you were in First Class) liner ever launched. What happened, though, was no surprise to any seaman. Joseph Conrad, responding to the formal inquiry into the sinking of the ship, was exasperated, and literal: 'the ship scraped her side against a piece of ice, and sank after floating for two hours and a half, taking a lot of people down with her.'

Thomas Hardy took a similar line: if you have a genuinely immovable object, it will scupper an allegedly irresistible force. His 1915 poem 'The Convergence of the Twain: Lines on the Loss of the *Titanic*' is an appropriate epitaph for both that great ship, and for Sangorski's Omar:

Jewels in joy designed
To ravish the sensuous mind
Lie lightless, all their sparkles bleared and black and blind.

Vanity, all is vanity. Like Conrad, who recoiled at the 'vulgar demand of a few moneyed people for a banal hotel luxury', Hardy's focus is on the colossal extravagance of the *Titanic*, and its collision (or convergence) with the iceberg attains an eerie moral inevitability. No mention is made of the loss of life.

The loss of the Great Omar, like the loss of the *Titanic*, teases the mind with questions about how such a fate might have been averted. The great bindery that created the *Rubaiyat*, having preserved the elaborate designs, was immediately anxious to produce another copy. No one was likely to raise the *Titanic*, but Sangorski and Sutcliffe could resurrect their Omar. Within two weeks, the firm wrote a letter to the *Telegraph:*

We, as designers and binders of this book have pleasure in stating that all the designs were copyrighted by us, and are still in our possession; and we would beg to point out that instead of working to no definite plan the work was executed from working designs every detail of which is recorded ... it is quite possible for us to reproduce the whole work.

But tragedy followed tragedy: On 1 July 1912, some ten weeks after the ship sank, Francis Sangorski, while bathing in the sea at Selsey Bay in Sussex, went bravely to the rescue of a woman who was drowning. He saved her life but was himself sucked under by the current, and died at the age of thirty-seven.

His widow, Frances, was left with four young children. For a time she worked for the firm, which was now being steered steadily through the war years by the capable George Sutcliffe, who, though lacking the genius of his former partner, continued to produce elaborate jewelled bindings. Indeed, during the first year of the war the bindery sold that jewelled copy of Keats's *Some Poems* for £1,400, a sum that confirmed that the Omar had been fairly priced by Sotheran's, and must have made Gabriel Weiss regret having dithered about his purchase of it, for, had he bought it in the first instance, it surely would have survived.

Curiously, when a second *Omar* was finally made, even George Sutcliffe didn't know about it. His nephew, the immensely able Stanley Bray, who had access to the original designs, conceived the notion of making another copy on his own, after returning from work each day at the bindery. It took him seven years, and was finished in 1939.

But the Second World War was then inevitable, and the securely packaged book was placed in a bank vault in the City of London. Two years later, after heavy bombing of the City, and a resulting spate of fierce fires driven by wind, the book was destroyed, literally melting in the heat. All that was left – Thomas Hardy would have appreciated this – was the jewels, which were later rescued from their congealed leather binding. In John Stonehouse's sad appraisal, 'a fatality seemed to follow the book.' Or perhaps the book caused the fatality? 'I come like water, and like the wind, I go', as Omar put it.

But it was curiously determined not to be lost to the

world, the Sangorski Omar, anxious to be reborn. Towards the end of his life Stanley Bray attempted yet another copy, which can now be found at the British Library, though it is less distinguished than the 1911 version.

It wasn't until 1998, when his firm moved offices to Bankside, that Rob Shepherd, searching for the first time through the archive of the old firm of Sangorski and Sutcliffe, discovered that the complete designs for the 1911 *Rubaiyat* had unexpectedly been preserved. It was, he says, 'an unforgettable experience', which confirmed in full detail just how magnificent a work the original binding had been. The records were complete: the preliminary sketches and a full book of Sangorski's tooling patterns and designs were accompanied by a set of glass negatives of the binding, and the original black-and-white photographs of it. Everything you would need, if the right commission were offered, to make yet another copy.

Alas, there are no more John Stonehouses in the rare book world, but there are still avid collectors of such material. If any of them has the requisite £333,000, the Great Omar might just rise again.

It's a nice thought, but it isn't likely to happen. There are plenty of collectors, of both rare books and of fine bindings, who could afford such a price, but the binding that Sangorski so triumphantly provided for the Great Omar is now an anachronism which has to be appreciated in its historical context, as Rob Shepherd acknowledges:

To some modern eyes, its opulence and excessive decoration seem rather absurd, but in the context of Edwardian England, Sangorski's extravagant interpretation of

Khayyam's verses fits perfectly with the spirit of his time. The First World War brought that period of opulence to an abrupt end, but the book remains a potent symbol of the innocence and confidence of those pre-War years. After 1918, the world is a very different place.

Who knows? The world is different in 2013 as well, and a new taste (and capacity to buy) such treasures may well be found – who understands such things? – amongst the Russian oligarchs who eat Fabergé eggs for breakfast, Indian mega-businessmen who spend tens of millions marrying off their daughters, Arab oil sheiks tired of buying football clubs or Chinese entrepreneurs who already own Shanghai. Such people are now the most active clientele of the major auction houses, with bejewelled wives and mistresses, fancy mansions, helicopters and yachts, and their demand for expensive gewgaws seems limitless. Bling-seekers enter the world of books?

It's not merely members of the press and public who have such stereotyped fantasies of the fabulous wealth, vulgarity and limitless appetites of the billionaires of the emerging nations; we book dealers have them as well. A few years ago I was approached by a representative of a Russian oligarch, and requested – *required* might be more accurate – that I find him '*Lolita* with inscription to wife'. I presumed he meant Vera, Vladimir's wife, though I did harbour the suspicion that he wanted me to get the long-dead Nabokov to do one specially for his Missus, maybe as a Valentine's Day gift. Presuming the former, within two weeks I had a copy to put in front of him, consisting of the first American edition, published by Putnam's in 1958, inscribed to Vera (to whom the book is dedicated) with a lovely example of one of the coloured butterfly drawings with which Nabokov adorned inscriptions to his closest friends and relations.

I had the book on consignment, for a period of three weeks only, from the late Dmitri Nabokov, the author's son, heir and literary executor. It was, to be frank, a most unprepossessing volume, a sad example of the low stand-ards of American book design and production in the 1950s. The dust wrapper was dowdy, dull and slightly fraying, the typography lifeless, the total effect a direct contradiction of the extraordinary vivacity and power of the contents. My Russian oligarch, shown the book by his representative, was not exactly overwhelmed. The book without the inscription was worth $50, and I was asking £250,000. A big premium for a few lines, however fond, to the wife, and a drawing of a pretty insect?

I had, of course, anticipated this perfectly reasonable response, and before showing the book to my oligarch, had obtained a letter from Sotheby's confirming that, if they were to offer the book at auction, it would be estimated at between £200,000 and £300,000. My putative customer was unimpressed by this as well. After some complex negotia-tions, though, I bought the book myself, and did indeed enter it into the next 'Russian Sale' at Sotheby's. I was by then wary of the 'it may be desirable, but it looks like shit' response. Oligarchs presumably need something that appeals to the eye. The answer: commission a bindery to make a drop-dead fancy leather box to put the book in. Head for Sangorski and Sutcliffe!

True to their origins, the firm came up with an *opulent*, eye-catching design for the box, with multicoloured leather inlays of butterflies all over it, each trailing streams of (real) gold dust. I had no idea if the price of £5,200 was reasonable or not, but I paid it. The Sotheby's catalogue entry for the sale made as much fuss of the box as they did of the book. A superb association copy in a fabulous box! Fit for a king, or an oligarch!

Wrong. On the day, as my wife, Belinda, and I sat in the audience crossing our fingers, there was not a single bid for the book. After some months it ended up, at a lower price, with an American collector who had no interest in the box at all. Presumably he now keeps matches in it. So even the services of the fabled Sangorski bindery could not drum up a customer for my book. It led me to wonder how many people really do buy bling bindings and boxes. How does the market in jewelled bindings work, if it does at all?

The answer, according to Peter Selley, of Sotheby's Book Department in London, is a small but active number of English, American and continental collectors – *not* wily Orientals or bloated oligarchs – whose interests are relatively similar. They tend to look, first, at what the text is – a collected poems of a major poet, an important novel, a famous private press book and (of course) an *Omar Khayyam*. The choices are, in general, obvious: it would be an odd person who wanted a jewelled binding on a Penguin original, or a copy of the latest Man Booker Prize winner. If you are investing heavily in the cover, you have to make sure that the contents are worth it.

But the binding is the key, and collectors are most sensitive to the quality and nature of the binding itself. According to Selley

I would say generally that there are some dedicated collectors in this area … and they intend to be selective about which bindings they buy. It is not like earlier periods, when Sangorski or other binders could put a nice binding on any work, and expect to be able to sell it handsomely.

Thus, in recent years, two different copies of William Morris's Kelmscott Press *Works of Geoffrey Chaucer* have come under the hammer. One of the fabled press books of the nineteenth century, and worth some £30,000 in its original binding, the jewelled copies fetched between two and four times that, depending on the opulence (that word again!) of the binding. Numerous *Omar*s have also passed through the auction rooms in the last ten years, most of them bound by Sangorski and Sutcliffe, who have more or less cornered the market.

The Great Omar, and Sangorski's fascination with the glories of the East, have left a telling legacy in the regular examples of jewelled copies that still flow out of his bindery. He was a great and visionary bookbinder, whose taste may now seem antique, but who continues to have his devoted, wealthy followers.

I wish they collected Nabokov.

11

Lost to the World: The Library of Guido Adler

There are too many easy assumptions about the improving qualities of art. Many of us have been encouraged to believe that literature (for example) can provide us with moral guidance. Latterly, it is widely claimed that reading is *in itself* good for us. Reading, we are told, enables us to determine the difference if not between right and wrong, at least between the serious and the frivolous. An analogous claim is frequently made about music. In listening well, one learns to refine one's judgements and deepen one's emotional responses, and in so doing is oneself refined. It sounds great, but unfortunately it's nonsense. That's clear enough when we remember those stressed-out Nazis, relaxing after a hard day, playing Wagner to soothe their savage breasts. When even that most moving of hymns to the brotherhood of man, Beethoven's setting of Schiller's *Ode to Joy*, was appropriated by Hitler.

Let me begin by citing a song, not in the hope that it will improve you, but because it is the basis, and the cause, of much that is to follow. Widely regarded as one of Mahler's finest lieder, *Ich bin der Welt abhanden gekommen* ('I am Lost to the World') is a setting of a poem by Friedrich Rückert:

I am lost to the world
With which I used to waste so much time,
It has heard nothing from me for so long,
That it may very well believe me dead!
It is of no importance to me,
Whether it thinks me dead;
I cannot deny it,
For I really am dead to the world.
I have died to the world's tumult
And rest in the realm of quiet.
I live alone in my own heaven,
In my love, in my song.

Mahler later observed that the song has an 'unusually concentrated and restrained style, is brim-full with emotion but does not overflow'. It was, he proclaimed, 'my very self!'

The orchestral version was first performed in Vienna in late January 1905, and on 1 November Mahler presented its manuscript to the eminent musicologist Guido Adler, with the warm inscription 'To my dear friend Guido Adler (who will certainly never be lost to me) as a memento of his fiftieth birthday'. Adler was overwhelmed by the gift, as the song cycle from which it came had particular meaning for him. The songs, he observed, 'embrace nature, the world of children and adults in the most diverse moods of love, profane and sacred, the most complete devotion descending by degrees to resignation, which achieves expression in the most luminous manner in the incomparable *Ich bin der Welt abhanden gekommen*'.

It is not clear what the monetary value of the manuscript would have been at the time, but Mahler was recognised

A Nazi officer superintends the loading of looted Jewish artworks.

as a composer of the first rank (he had already completed seven symphonies), and it was certain to be of substantial value in the future. Rather than putting it in a drawer in his magnificent library, Adler put it in the safe where his greatest treasures were held, which included one of only three known copies of Beethoven's death mask, as well as letters by Brahms and Bruckner.

Guido Adler began life as one of those precocious children that were so common in nineteenth century *mittel*-European culture. As a student at the Conservatory in Vienna, this earnest, aspirational boy once had the honour of introducing a recital by Franz Liszt, who kindly kissed him on the forehead while holding his hands. Guido, overcome, preserved the gloves he wore that night, regarding them as 'precious relics'.

It's a common enough process and feeling. After all, people do the same today, though with regard to the by-products of rock stars or football players rather than classical composers. The possession of the 'precious relic' – whether it is the Lisztified glove or Napoleonic relic, John Lennon's guitar or Pelé's number 10 football shirt – conveys to the recipient, in an alchemical transfer, some of the power and authority of the donor. One can imagine the boy Guido pressing the gloves to his lips, and feeling himself instantly transformed into something, and *someone*, bigger and better.

This is simultaneously funny, and sad, and ominous. Perhaps it is because so many of these swooning Teutonic wannabe geniuses were soon to swell the ranks of the Third Reich, a sure sign that high culture, whatever it is and does, does not necessarily humanise. Some thirty-odd years later poor Guido Adler, so like his fellow students and scholars, with such commonality of interest, was to become a victim of his musicological colleagues, because (unlike many of them) he was a Jew.

Guido had wanted to become a composer, and though competent by professional standards, he had to acknowledge that he was untouched by any genius – other than Liszt – and became a scholar instead. It was, he later remarked, the hardest decision of his life: 'I was and am of the opinion that those who cannot contribute something new had better stay silent.'

But this modest disclaimer masks the fact that Guido Adler certainly did contribute 'something new', and was far from silent. He is frequently regarded as the first musicologist, and his ground-breaking article of 1885 'The Scope, Method and Goals of Musicology' set the method and aims of this new subject. In it, Adler distinguishes between the historical and systematic study of music, and his contributions to the ensuing development of the subject have been described as the work of a 'firebrand, bringing to the world of scholarship a vision of a new field'.

By the time he retired, in 1927, Guido Adler was among the foremost modern musicologists, and the luminary of the Institute of Musicology at the University of Vienna. The author or editor of a number of seminal books, including the eighty volumes of *Monuments of Music in Austria*, Herr Hofrat Professor Doktor Adler had every reason to look forward to a happy and productive retirement.

But by the time of the publication of his memoirs, in 1935, the shadows were deeply cast, and many Jews were leaving Austria. As the pressures on Viennese Jews intensified, Guido encouraged his son, daughter-in-law and their children to depart for America, but continued to hope for the best, and made no plans to get out. American friends offered to pay his fare, and that of his eccentric and dutiful daughter Melanie, who, dressed as a man, frequently went missing on mysterious assignations, accumulated a curiously large amount of money (considering she never worked) and was prone to her own bouts of anti-Semitism. She was something of a puzzle and an embarrassment to her own family, and her mother's wry remark – 'she does certain things we're not talking about' – hints, perhaps, at a covert lesbian life, enacted far from home, in the licentious hot spots of Berlin and Munich.

As things worsened in Vienna, Guido and his daughter applied for, and were eventually granted, exit visas, but when the moment came, he found he simply could not leave. 'The old Adler,' he remarked – 'Adler' means 'eagle' in German – 'the old Adler has grown tired of flying.' He had an understandable unwillingness, at the age of eighty-two, to relocate himself in a trying new life in America. Of course, he did not know what was to come, however ominous the signs, and even at the time of his death was blessedly unaware of the full scope of the unfolding tragedy.

Melanie remained in Austria out of daughterly devotion to her father, Guido out of attachment to his library. He had spent most of a lifetime building it, and aside from the remarkable depth of the book collection, it had in it those 'precious relics', such as the Mahler manuscript, through which he had, since boyhood, partly defined himself. It is, as many contemporary Jews found to their cost, a dangerous process to bind oneself to one's objects.

Guido Adler died of natural causes in 1941, at the age

of eighty-six. He was lucky. He had hardly been laid to rest when the cultured vultures moved in. Though the library now belonged to Melanie, and represented her only bargaining chip in avoiding the Gestapo, she was powerless to avoid its systematic looting. One of Guido's former students, the Director of the Music Collection of the City of Vienna, confiscated a large number of rare volumes on behalf of that happy institution. A second famous musicologist, Guido's former colleague Professor Erich Schenk, an ardent Nazi posing as a family friend, offered Melanie an exit visa to Italy in exchange for the contents of the library. She demurred, seeking both a better and a more secure deal, in spite of the counsel of her appointed lawyer, Richard Heiserer, who urged her to accept Schenk's offer.

As Jews were no longer allowed to practise law, Heiserer specialised in dealing with the property of Jewish clients, a lucrative field for a lawyer who was a member in particularly good standing of the Nazi party. A Nazi Party district report gave him good marks: his 'conduct toward the party and the state is impeccable. He spent a lot for the party, and eagerly. His personal assets are very substantial. He behaves socially to the other party comrades.'

This risible claptrap makes it clear why Heiserer was valued, and there can be no doubt that his 'personal assets' were accumulated as a result of unscrupulous practice. Demanding the only set of keys to her father's library from the grieving Melanie, Heiserer effectively took complete control of its contents. Frightened but fighting back, Melanie tried instead to sell the books to the Munich City Library. When this fell through, she made a desperate final appeal to Richard Wagner's daughter-in-law Winifred, who was born in England but had moved to Germany as a child, and was both an ardent admirer and personal friend of Hitler. The Führer – whom she called 'Wolf' – was close to Winifred's children, and there was some gossip of a relationship between the pair. Nevertheless, she opposed the brutality of the rise to power of the Nazis – for which she did not hold Hitler personally responsible, though she challenged him on the subject – and was well known for her acts of charity.

Melanie's letter to Winifred, who knew the family slightly, is desperately painful and grovelling, as if made by a peasant supplicant to an empress, begging for her life to be spared (which is more or less what it is). It begins 'Most revered, merciful Lady' and thanks Winifred (who had previously helped her to continue residence in the family home, when most Jews had been moved out of theirs and into a ghetto): 'what remains is only my large, large gratitude and reverence for you, honourable and merciful lady!'

Offering Guido's entire library in exchange for the chance to move to Munich (why she regarded that city as safe is unclear), Melanie Adler had made her final plea. Her attorney, she noted, was 'threatening me with the Gestapo in order to intimidate me'. But Winifred was unwilling or unable to help her, naïvely unaware of how bad things really were, and nothing came of this final appeal.

Heiserer wasn't bluffing. Melanie tried to fire him, but it was too late. She was repeatedly 'interviewed' by the Gestapo, and the contents of the library were systematically pillaged. In May 1942 Melanie Adler was transported to Minsk, and thence to a lonely pine forest outside Maly Trostinec. Of the 9,000 people sent to that killing ground, only seventeen survived. The rest were shot, and buried in mass graves.

Most of what was most valuable in Guido's library had disappeared, though after the war the remnants were inherited by his son, who had relocated to America with his family and sold them to the University of Georgia in 1951. No one knew what had happened to the most valuable items from of the library of Guido Adler. No one could locate the manuscript of *I am Lost to the World*.

Some fifty years later, in September 2000, Tom Adler, a California lawyer who was Guido's grandson, received an email informing him that the lost Mahler manuscript, with its dedication to Guido Adler, had been located, and was presently being appraised at Sotheby's office in Vienna. Ironically, Tom Adler, who had recently retired, had been devoting more and more of his time to trying to find out what had happened to his grandfather's possessions, in the hope that by tracking the things the history of his family might also become clearer (a compelling recent example of this very process can be found in Edmund de Waal's *The Hare with Amber Eyes*).

That this was a particularly significant moment – not merely in terms of the value of the manuscript – was clear when Adler was told the name of its consignor: Richard Heiserer, the son of the lawyer who had 'represented' Melanie Adler. Heiserer had no doubt that he had title to the disputed manuscript: his father, he claimed, 'got Mahler's musical piece in a legal way probably as compensation for the work he did as appointed lawyer to Dr Guido Adler'.

It was inconceivable that Melanie would have given her father's most precious possession to the lawyer the Nazis had foisted on her to deal with the probate of the estate. Within a few weeks Tom Adler and Richard Heiserer (who had 'inherited' the manuscript at the age of fourteen) were face to face, as their forebears had been some sixty years earlier. Heiserer would neither look Adler in the eye nor shake his hand. The manuscript, he insisted frostily, had been given to his father as payment for services rendered in 'a legal way', and though there was no paperwork to support this allegation, it had no doubt been lost during the chaos of the post-war years. Fortunately the manuscript itself had not been lost to the world, and Heiserer junior had no intention of allowing it – or its monetary equivalent – being lost to him.

It was a rotten moral position and a shaky legal argument, but Austria's laws on the subject of reparations have been weak and ambiguous. The unwillingness to provide proper compensation for its treatment of the Jews and the wholesale looting of their property has been shameful, and it took over fifty years for the state to accept full responsibility for its crimes. Though the war had been lost, most post-war Austrians continued their habitual anti-Semitism. Ex-Nazis were granted an amnesty as early as 1948 (one of them, Kurt Waldheim, subsequently became the country's President), and in the same year a poll showed that about half the population believed that the Jews had caused their own fate, and 'something had to be done to place limits on them'. There was certainly no national will to acknowledge how repellent the situation not only had been but continued to be.

Gestures were made. By 1947 there had already been three Restitution Acts, but they were hedged about with significant reservations. Though the Third Act recognised that all property taken by the Nazis had been obtained illegally, the holder of any contested property had to show that it had been appropriated under the Nazi regime. Any new 'owner' who could claim that he had been unaware that the property had been illegally seized was under no obligation to return it. In any case, all claims for restitution had to be made within nine years – a time insufficient both practically (discoveries of such property went on for many decades) and morally. Why should such a time limit be imposed?

The reason may lie – as a confidential US State Department memo of 1950 noted – in the fact that the Austrian government was itself complicit in the storage and covert dissemination of many thousands of items of dubious provenance. According to Tom Adler – whose account of his grandfather's library is an invaluable source – 'of the more than $1 billion worth of Jewish assets taken by the Austrians under the Nazi regime … only a small portion was returned to Jewish owners and heirs.'

In 1998 – two generations since the end of the war! – the Austrian government finally passed a law that required the return of all art work taken by the Nazis which 'entered museums and art collections under questionable circumstances'. Under this new ruling, though still with the usual difficulties regarding title, many exceedingly important pictures were returned to their rightful owners. The Rothschild family, alone, recovered more than 250 works of art.

It was only two years later that Tom Adler began his battle to retrieve Guido's Mahler manuscript, by which time the tide of feeling and legislation in Austria had – at last – caught up with the imperatives of international law and feeling. Indeed, once it was noted that the Mahler manuscript might be described as having been looted during the war, an export licence was immediately granted. The details have not been revealed, but after protracted legal wrangling Tom Adler retrieved his family manuscript, and Sotheby's went ahead with the sale in London. Their catalogue description makes reference to the dispute, noting that 'the manuscript is now the sole property of Mr Tom Adler, Guido Adler's grandson, following a court-approved settlement with the Heiserer family', which suggests that some money must have changed hands. I hope it wasn't much.

On 21 May 2004, *I am Lost to the World* – described as 'one of the greatest autograph manuscripts of Mahler ever offered for sale at auction' – was sold for £420,000 in London, to a private collector (it is now on deposit at the Morgan Library in New York). I trust the buyer has learned the full story. Because what they purchased is not just a musical treasure but an artefact soaked in blood, and perfidy, and love. It carries the dreadful story of the musicologist and his devoted daughter, in which a poignant sliver of the history of those terrible times is recovered. It is essential that such stories, like musical manuscripts, never be lost to the world.

Art theft, in its many forms, is a gigantic industry and occurs over a wide spectrum, from Picasso's casual thefts from the Louvre in search of inspiring objects, through Vincenzo Peruggia's curiously innocent and likeable theft of the *Mona Lisa*, including the political appropriation of art objects (as in the theft of the Urewera mural in New Zealand) right through to the palpable wickedness of Richard Heiserer's pillaging of Guido Adler's library.

Today, art theft is the world's third largest criminal industry, exceeded in total value only by arms and drug dealing. The FBI estimates that some $6 billion worth of art – in

Donald Rumsfeld's phrase, 'who would have thought there were so many vases?' – is stolen *every year*. 'It's Like Stealing History', proclaims the FBI website, and one can only regret the unnecessary simile. It *is* stealing history.

The rise in contemporary art theft (the value of which doubled between 2001 and 2011) is due to a number of factors. First, of course, the art market has exploded over that period, with spectacular auction prices (the era of the $100 million dollar painting has now arrived) widely publicised, and hence providing temptation to art thieves. And as art becomes more valuable, so too is awareness of art theft, so that more crimes are reported to the police. Robert Wittman, a former FBI agent, notes that 'Art crime is on the rise because it is basically an economic crime. Art is one of the safe havens at this point, as far as assets are concerned, and criminals are not immune to seeing that in the papers and seeing the rise in auction prices.'

There is a prevalent belief, unsupported by much evidence, that much art is stolen to order by anonymous and reclusive wealthy art collectors, anxious to make illicit additions to their holdings. In fact, though, most stolen art is either sold foolishly into the art trade at a bargain price, or held to ransom, where insurance companies, keen to avoid a big payout, will often pay a low percentage (sometimes as low as 10 per cent) of a work's value to recover it.

Art thieves are audacious, but their nerve is often unaccompanied by any clear idea of how to profit from their crimes. Most stolen objects find a fence easily enough, because they are not unique, but important works of art have usually been photographed and recorded, and are not easy to dispose of. Even if the stolen works are held back for many years – as in the case of the Mahler manuscript – when they appear they are likely to be recognised.

Wittman makes the point crisply:

> Thieves may be good criminals, but they're often terrible businessmen. Most are common criminals who will steal anything. In all other crime there is no problem in monetising the loot: if you steal drugs or jewellery, you get money. You can chop up a car and sell it for parts. You can't shift a stolen Picasso.

Or a stolen *I am Lost to the World*, even after sixty years. Great art may not to be easy to protect from opportunist pilfering, but it is hard to dispose of, and has a pleasing way of returning to its rightful place, and owner.

12

Lumps of Coal: The Destruction of the Library at Herculaneum

Sometimes a story, no matter how compelling, can become so well known that it becomes almost impossible to imagine freshly. Take the sinking of the *Titanic*. Majestic new ship, maiden voyage, fancy passengers, jewels galore, iceberg, band plays on, gurgle, gurgle. As that dreadful film demonstrated, there's no longer enough to arrest your attention here, even with the undoubted appeal of the death by drowning of Leonardo DiCaprio.

Similarly, it is hard to get an interesting angle on the eruption of Vesuvius, and the resulting destruction of Pompeii and Herculaneum in AD 79. Robert Harris's brilliant novel on the subject filters the story through an obscure Roman water engineer, faced with the perplexing problem of why the local water supply is failing. Even though we know what this presages, the point of view holds our attention better than bubbling streams of molten lava and hordes of overheated citizens.

I wish I'd thought of that. But when I reflect about the eruption of Vesuvius – which, admittedly, is not very often – all that comes to mind, sadly, is lumps of coal.

To explain, I need to move a few miles up the coast, once the site of the prosperous town of Herculaneum. Here lived a Roman Senator, Lucius Calpurnius Piso, the father-in-law of Julius Caesar, in a residence so fancy that it was later to serve as the model for the first Getty Museum. Stretching some 250 metres along the shoreline, the villa was a repository of the arts, the occasional resting place of philosophers, including the Epicurean Philodemus, and the home of one of the finest private libraries of Classical antiquity, made up of thousands of manuscript scrolls written on papyrus, a wetland sedge which had first been used for writing on in ancient Egypt. This vegetable material, properly prepared, took ink very well, but was unlikely to have a protracted life, being subject to decay if exposed to overly wet or dry conditions.

It is hard to imagine a grander place to live than this, the vast expanse of the sea fronting the villa, and the majesty of Mount Vesuvius only some seven miles behind it, to the west. Life may have been supremely comfortable in such a setting, but it was also likely, even in these exalted ranks, to be dangerous and often short. There were constant threats of war, and potentially mortal illnesses were difficult to diagnose and almost impossible to treat. There was medicine and surgery, to be sure, as the grisly implements from scalpels to forceps that survive from this period (at the House of the Surgeon in Pompeii) testify, but in the absence of any adequate form of anaesthesia it is hard to imagine that serious surgery was much preferable to death. The average lifespan was less than forty years, and what one was fortunate enough to have by way of life, and health, and pleasure was certainly to be celebrated. A philosophical school – precursors in their way of Omar Khayyam – was founded to do just this.

The original of this building lies under many metres of volcanic detritus; it has been recreated as The Getty Museum in Malibu, where its brash newness makes it look like an upmarket Hilton.

But even Epicurus, and his follower Philodemus, could not have imagined any catastrophe so likely to divert mind and body from life's pleasures as the eruption of Mount Vesuvius on 24 August AD 79. The scene was described with remarkable power by Pliny the Younger, who was there, putting it all down with his characteristic precision and elegance, in a letter he sent to Tacitus about twenty-five years after the event:

> A cloud was forming ... Its appearance and shape would be best expressed as being that of an umbrella pine. Since, stretched upward like an extremely tall tree trunk, it then spread out like branches ... Sometimes it was white, sometimes dirty and blotchy, because of the soil or ash that it carried.

Rightly terrified by the appearance of this sinister cloud, which blotted out the sun, and the resounding shocks of earthquakes and bolts of lightning, the townspeople of the two threatened cities reacted differently. To the south, Pompeii (which was downwind of the explosion) was bombarded by rocks and heated material that made going out into the street and towards the boats extremely hazardous; in Herculaneum there was a better chance of survival from the ash falls by fleeing outdoors, but that was a thoroughly disagreeable option. Most people stayed inside, and died.

As conditions worsened dramatically, Pliny's uncle's life was in danger:

> Soon great flames and vast fires shone from many points on Mount Vesuvius, the gleam and the light made more vivid by the night time shadows ... Supported by two slaves,

he stood up but immediately fell down again, because, I suppose, the air, thickened with ash, had obstructed his breathing and blocked his windpipe, which was delicate and narrow by nature and frequently inflamed. When daylight returned (the third day after he had breathed his last) his body was found intact and unharmed ... He was more like a man sleeping than one who was dead.

Within a few days of the first eruption, the sea had receded hundreds of feet, and the town of Herculaneum was buried under smouldering rock – the pyroclastic flow – to a depth of 70 feet. It is hard to imagine a more comprehensive destruction of what lay underneath.

Yet, curiously, the eruption of Vesuvius may well have been the best thing that could have happened to the manuscripts of the Villa of the Papyri, as it came to be known. The manuscripts may have been carbonised, and encased in rock, but they were preserved, whereas no other papyrus manuscripts from this period have survived. All somebody had to do was find them and (what is admittedly harder) figure out a way to read them in their new form.

It wasn't until 1709 that some workmen, boring a water hole, came upon the mosaic floor of the buried villa beneath. They had unwittingly dropped into the finest site of ancient Roman artefacts yet uncovered. For many years the underground villa was systematically tunnelled and unsystematically looted: the King of Naples filled his palaces and museums, individual robbers carried away myriad examples of marble and bronze statuary.

Some time in 1752 the looters – they could hardly be classed as archaeologists – came across what they first conceived to be oddly shaped lumps of coal, or perhaps carbonised tree branches, crushed by pressure and distorted by moisture. At first, they were a useful source of fuel and light in the dank conditions, but it wasn't long before some observant soul noticed that the chunks of blackened matter had writing on them. A systematic collection of the objects ensued, and 1,800 examples were brought up to the surface, and taken to Naples for analysis. They soon proved to be the remnants of the only surviving library of the ancient world.

Two contradictory things then happened, almost simultaneously. First, there was constant and increasingly acrimonious squabbling between Spain, Italy and England regarding custodianship of the newly emerged material. And secondly, as soon as the papyri began to be, however inadequately, deciphered, most analysts agreed in their disappointment with the contents. To have waited so long, and to have worked so hard at unravelling ... this? Altogether too many minor Epicurean tracts: several commentators speculated that no more than 10 per cent of the find was likely to be of interest, if it could ever be transcribed.

Imagine the frustration. Here, obviously, was an archaeological find of some significance, a glimpse back to the Roman world of the first century. Various methods were tried to unroll and decipher the rolls: some were slit in half and picked at with a knife (and largely disintegrated); liquid mercury was poured over others; Sir Humphry Davy came from England with a theory about chemical solvents. Nothing worked. As there was nothing to practise on, and science proceeds through trial and error, there were a lot of trials and as many errors. Maybe this would work? Or that? The result was a significant loss of carbonised papyrus rolls.

As some sixty years passed, the papyri deteriorated and disappeared at an alarming rate. They were given away as gifts by the King of Naples (Napoleon got some, and a couple ended up at Oxford), and eighteen were swapped for an equal number of kangaroos. (It seemed a fair deal: the papyri were unreadable, and the kangaroos manky and disease-ridden.)

In time, though, a method was evolved for slowly opening them, and attaching the delicate remains of the papyrus to an animal membrane. Though the process was crude and painstaking – the first unravelling of a single scroll took four years – increasing numbers of the papyri were eventually laid out ready to be read. To imagine this, you have to envisage myriad tiny burned potato crisps, each of such delicacy that a mere touch of the finger would turn it to dust, and curved so that its surfaces reflected the light in different ways. Black ink on blackened material, in the worst conceivable condition. Occasional words, tantalisingly, could be made out. A phrase here and there. Enough to confirm that the find was not unimportant, if frustratingly elusive.

The saved, if depleting, store of papyri, and the possibility of many others still underground, was of such intense interest to classicists and archaeologists because shadowing their enthusiasm was the collective memory of that immense loss, the great library at Alexandria. Piso's library was that of a wealthy and enthusiastic amateur, and reflected his passions – largely the Epicureans – and contained what was reasonably available. But his holdings were tiny and relatively insignificant compared to those of the greatest library of Classical antiquity.

Alexander the Great, who created what was to become an

immense and wealthy city, the trading hub of the ancient world, had it as one of the aims of empire to appropriate the accumulated wisdom of all the cultures he conquered and to establish a setting in which every available book in the world might be found. The library itself was established by a former student of Aristotle's, under the reign of Alexander's successor, Ptolemy Soter (*c*. 367–*c*. 283 BC). It was a fabulous resource: Aristotle's surviving library, for instance, provided part of the initial holdings at Alexandria.

The goal was to put into one place all the available works that mankind had produced, translate them into Greek, arrange them systematically and make them available for study. Ptolemy Soter and his immediate successors were, without question, the greatest book collectors in the history of the world, for the history of the world was what they were collecting, and they were insatiable and unscrupulous in their acquisition of everything that had been written. What they could not acquire through conquest they purchased, stole, or borrowed. For centuries after, the library was the greatest repository of human knowledge of the ancient world; indeed, no library since has been able to claim to hold such a high percentage of the world's available intellectual treasures.

It was a beautiful establishment, as well as a useful one. Standing next to the Mouseion (or Museum) in grounds like that of a modern university campus, scholars were given well-paid jobs for life under the (sometimes wilful) patronage of the King. There were botanical and zoological gardens, winding paths, colonnades and courtyards, in homage to the Aristotelian idea of the peripatetic pursuit of knowledge. An outdoor amphitheatre (the *exedra*) served as an equivalent of a college auditorium or theatre, a space set aside for lectures and performances.

Conditions were generally peaceful and beautiful, and the project astonishingly ambitious, energetic and well funded. But there were, of course, critics. There are always critics where academic life goes on, and intellectual foment occurs. Timon of Phlius derided the bibliophiles 'scribbling endlessly and waging a constant war of words with each other' in exactly the same terms as modern critics of academic squabbling.

Commentators are agreed that the hundreds of thousands of scrolls which were systematically collected – and created – at Alexandria perished in a fire. But there is no consensus as to who or what started the fire, or, indeed, when it occurred. Most accounts blame Julius Caesar, during his siege of the city in 48 BC. According to Plutarch: 'when the enemy endeavoured to cut off his communication by sea, he was forced to divert that danger by setting fire to his own ships, which, after burning the docks, thence spread on and destroyed the great library.' Other commentators have ascribed the loss of the library to different fires, at different times, and some (probably wrongly) believe it survived until its destruction by the forces of Caliph Omar some time around AD 640.

But whenever it happened, the one certainty is that the scrolls from the Alexandria library perished irretrievably, unlike the carbonised examples from the Villa of the Papyri. When – at last – a Polish–Egyptian archaeological team could make a reasonable claim to have discovered the site and ruins of the great library at Alexandria, in 2004, there was scant chance that anything of the written records would have survived. Ashes, long dispersed, only ashes. Nothing as substantial as carbon.

By a wonderful historical irony, the breakthrough that allowed the reading of the carbonised manuscripts from Piso's villa was a result of technology pioneered by that colossal waste of money, the NASA space programme. When viewed under multi-spectral imaging infra-red light at between 900 and 950 nanometres, the carbonised papyri of Herculaneum burst into clear legibility. When the results were revealed to that most jaded of audiences, a colloquium of Oxford dons, in 1999, they positively shrieked with delight, as the dead texts returned from their two thousand years of silence.

Over the last six years it has become clear what an important source the papyri are, and will be. The bulk of them, predictably, are works by Philodemus. The Villa of the Papyri was an ideal place for an Epicurean to hang out, eat well, enjoy life, do a little philosophising. The basis of their thinking, roughly, consisted of praise and justification not for the having, but for the eating, of one's cake.

This may strike you as trivial, or unworthy, but cake has had rather a hard time in Christian theology. We have been so keen on the life of the spirit or the mind, as opposed to the pressing imperatives of the body, so anxious to prepare for entry into a better world (in which cake doesn't figure), that it is heartening to hear an argument for the pleasures of this life, now. As a philosophical position it is appealing but limited, though it is surprising what a fuss can be made of it. Among the new manuscripts were dozens of works by Philodemus, which may put us in danger of knowing more about him than we care to.

Described by Dr Andrew Gow as 'pedestrian in style, earnest in tone, uninspired though not uninteresting in content', the major interest in these texts consist of those fragments in which Philodemus argues with Aristotle about the nature of poetry. But this rather staid philosopher – why weren't Epicureans more *fun*? – can be offset by quoting a poetic fragment found at Pompeii, almost certainly by the self-same philosopher, in praise of his mistress:

> She is always ready for
> Anything, and often lets
> Me have it free. I'll put up
> With Philainion,
> O golden Cypris, until
> A better one is invented.

Now that's more like it.

Other finds were remarkable: more than half of the works of Epicurus, and an unknown treatise of Philodemus' master, Zeno of Sidon (the first text of his ever to come to light), were also uncovered and brought back to life. As work went on in the 1990s, it became clear that the Villa of the Papyri was larger – much larger – than had been imagined. It is now estimated that at least two further unexcavated levels, perhaps some 30,000 square feet, are still underground. And there is a growing consensus that more papyri – perhaps the main bulk of them – were in a further library or libraries which have not yet been excavated. According to this theory, the 1,800 scrolls found at the higher level, and scattered about the floors, were probably being transported in crates, in the hope of saving them from the encroaching disaster. They may have been taken from the even more extensive treasury below.

But as keenly as one might wish these possible treasures investigated, there are sober voices arguing for calm. As Andrew Wallace-Hadrill, the Director of the Herculaneum Research Project, has observed, it is also a priority to preserve the excavated remains of the Villa, which are 'undergoing a conservation crisis – it's crumbling away. It's hard to believe if you didn't see it with your own eyes … to keep this delicate "reborn" patient alive is a massive challenge … Because of this crisis, I'm almost indifferent on the subject of the papyri.'

So there we have it. One, perhaps two further libraries, preserved but unexcavated. The classicists slavering, demanding texts; the politicians and archaeologists wondering what the hurry is. Those manuscripts certainly aren't going anywhere, and until the time is right, and the conditions above ground improved, surely the lost treasures of the Villa of the Papyri can wait?

It isn't a question of money, which has been made available by an American charity. The cost of recovering the buried manuscripts is estimated at something like $25 million, which (need I remind you?) is less than a professional sports team can pay for a good player. Add some more money, and you could do the necessary ground work as well. It's only a matter of priorities.

I suspect that the relatively leisurely pace of the excavations at Herculaneum is a direct response to how important the further buried material is conceived to be. Of the 1,800 recovered manuscripts, few could be described as finds of the highest importance, and God knows no one is clamouring for more texts by Philodemus.

Imagine, though, if the remains of the scrolls at Alexandria had been similarly carbonised. Ptolemy Soter had set a goal of collecting 500,000 scrolls, and it was impossible to land a ship in the harbour at Alexandria without surrendering any on-board scrolls to be copied for the burgeoning library collection. And if there were significant gaps in the collection, the library would attempt – in a sort of precursor of the inter-library loan – to borrow significant material from elsewhere.

Ptolemy III applied to Athens, according to Galen's account, for permission to borrow and to copy significant scrolls by the three great Greek tragedians, Aeschylus, Sophocles and Euripides. The Aeschylus papyri, for instance, being the only known transcription of the complete works, were of incalculable value, even then. Unwilling to part with such treasure without a significant ransom, the Athenians demanded a surety of some 15 talents (over 900 pounds of precious metals, worth many millions of dollars today) to guarantee the safe return of the scrolls. They were never returned (though copies of them were sent back to the Athenians), being reckoned to be worth more, even, than their ransom value, for it was presumably an enormous coup for the Alexandrians to hold original material of this kind.

Papyrus is a notably frangible material, and it is likely that, if fire hadn't destroyed the manuscripts at Alexandria, something else would have. What we have received as the literature and philosophy of the ancient world is but a tiny fragment of what once existed, and many of the greatest works from that period are irretrievably lost. As Stuart Kelly concludes, in his *The Book of Lost Books*, 'the entire history of literature is also the history of the loss of literature.'

It would be wrong-headed to claim much benefit from this loss. There are only seven surviving plays of Aeschylus (of a total of eighty), seven from Sophocles (from a probable thirty-three, though others have estimated as many as 123), eighteen (of ninety odd) from Euripides and hardly anything from other contemporary playwrights. What survives is esteemed so very highly, surely, not merely because of its inherent qualities, but because it is so little garnered from so much: a reminder of how delicate our cultural and artistic heritage is, and how much we have to do to preserve it.

13

So Many Vases:
The Cradle of Civilisation

It is called the 'cradle of civilisation'. Six thousand years ago, the fertile lands of Mesopotamia between the Tigris and Euphrates rivers (often posited as the location of the Garden of Eden) became the home of a succession of cultures – the Sumerians, Assyrians and Babylonians – which produced what is sometimes referred to as the 'first book' – the epic of Gilgamesh – and an immense variety of beautiful objects, many of which may be seen in museums round the world. It is a fabled territory, astonishing in the diversity of its stories, arts and sciences, the place where mathematics, astronomy and medicine were first practised.

Nowadays it is called Iraq, and it is a sad and sorry place. Yet no matter how horrific its recent history, even under the reviled Saddam Hussein, Iraqis are rightly proud of what they regard as their heritage, and their National Museum in Baghdad has long been recognised as one of the finest collections of Mesopotamian antiquities in the world.

Whether it still is, is uncertain. Closed after the Iraq War began in 2003, due to the widespread damage and looting that took place, its façade pockmarked with bullet holes and breached by a tank shell, the museum was unprotected because the one American tank that was in fact stationed in front of it apparently lacked clearance to retaliate or to intervene. The situation was so dangerous that the building was closed to all its staff – the only people with free entry were the looters – just as its Director, Donny George, had warned: 'if anything happens, then the Museum will be targeted.' He was soon to seek asylum abroad after receiving death threats.

His museum was under siege. It has been (conservatively) estimated that some 15,000 antiquities went missing, many of which have since appeared on the market in the West. Of these, thousands were so small and apparently untraceable that they simply disappeared. These consisted, as the *Guardian* was later to report, of:

> the little scraps of history, less beautiful but more precious to the experts: the poems and spells, star charts and family histories, shopping lists and tax bills inscribed on scruffy little lozenges of mudbrick or cough drop-sized cylinder seals, which seeped out through Iraq's borders into the world's antiquities markets.

While a heartening number of major pieces were eventually restored to the museum, being more recognisable and harder to sell, most of the remarkably resonant bits and pieces never had a chance. The curator Irving Finkel of the British Museum, an expert on Babylonian artefacts, said that he was 'not aware of any major recovery of these pieces … I'm not holding my breath for one.'

But there were some pleasing surprises, as thousands of

Collateral damage? Bush and Rumsfeld's soldiers lay waste to one of the treasures of ancient Mesopotamia.

works fell back into place, some of which had been removed for safe keeping, others of which had clearly been taken by locals who had second thoughts. An amnesty for looters speeded the process, though Sarah Collins, a curator at the British Museum who worked with the Iraqi Museum for several months after war ended in 2003, reported that many people returning artefacts still expected to be paid. They weren't. Paradoxically, though, she noted that such unrestrained looting was a relatively new phenomenon: it 'wasn't a problem under Saddam. He beheaded a couple of looters and that put a stop to it.' This wasn't strictly true – it would be amusing to regard it as a form of wish fulfilment – because Mesopotamian antiquities had been leaking out of Iraq for centuries, even under the strict policies of Saddam.

Among the most significant of the returned objects was the Warka Mask, a beautiful and mysterious image which is some 5,500 years old, and which after its theft had been buried (no one knew by whom) in a field outside Baghdad. It was thought to have been sold several times locally after it was stolen, but eventually the thieves realised that it was probably too well known to be saleable in the wider antiquities market. The equally important Warka Vase was similarly returned (in pieces), securely wrapped up in a blanket in the boot of a car. But for every such gain – or regain – there were commensurate losses, a great many of them untraceable because the museum contained so many uncatalogued pieces.

It is a tragedy, and a disgrace. It could well have been avoided. Both the Bush and Blair administrations had been warned, well in advance of the first strikes, that the museum needed to be protected. Neither government took the relatively simple necessary steps – a tank which was actually authorised to act, and a few tough-looking armed guards might have done the trick – and for days after the first incursion into the museum on 11 April looters were free to come and go as they liked, to take away anything that was even remotely transportable. In the darkness – Baghdad's electricity was down – 120 internal doors to the offices and galleries were crowbarred from their hinges, and even the furniture was removed, while much of the collection and records were carted off.

That's appalling, surely? Not to Donald Rumsfeld, the American Secretary of Defense, who was uninterested in these trivial collateral losses, merely remarking that 'democracy is messy'. When informed how messy, and how great was the loss, not just of human life but of art and antiquities, the indefatigably loathsome Rumsfeld reportedly informed colleagues that the war in Iraq was an absolutely necessary response to the attack on the Twin Towers on 9/11: 'There just aren't enough targets in Afghanistan. We need to bomb something else to prove we're, you know, big and strong and not going to be pushed around.' So what if museum and cultural artefacts were destroyed? Looking at pictures of the looting, Rumsfeld joked that 'it's the same picture of some person walking out of some building with a vase, and you've seen it twenty times and you think "My goodness, were there that many vases?" Is it possible that there were that many vases in the whole country?'

The modern history of the looting of Iraq begins with the Gulf War in 1991, and the imposition of United Nations trade sanctions, which had devastating effects, not all of which were intended. In the absence of international trade, with tourism virtually non-existent, ordinary Iraqis found themselves suffering more than their leaders, desperate to make a living. And any country with as rich an archaeological past as Iraq is going to be a hotbed of casual collection – call it looting if you wish to be severe – of the available detritus. 'The problem is, if you dig pretty much anywhere, you'll find something ancient and interesting', said an Interpol Agent from the Stolen Works of Art Department. The further problem was that 99 per cent of the objects uncovered in this haphazard manner were either damaged in the process or discarded as insufficiently saleable.

Shards of this and that, bits of cuneiform tablets and cylinder seals, broken pieces of sculpture, bricks, tiles, pottery – yes, including vases – were gathered up from holes as deep as swimming pools, and the best of them were sold through the covert antique trade and in local bazaars. At the ancient site of Umma, over 200 looters a day were regularly to be found, with their own electrical generators to aid night excavation, and an infrastructure of vendors to supply food, drink and cigarettes. But this was not merely a motley array of poor people literally scraping a living: terrorist groups, reportedly including Al Qaeda, Sunni insurgents and later the Shiite militias, apparently used the limitless supply of antiquities as a source of funds, while unscrupulous international antiquities dealers made rapacious use of the steady supply lines into and from Baghdad.

By the time the Iraq War started, there were already established conduits out of the country for saleable items. The West was soon flooded with material, and the only law impeding the looting of Iraq was that of supply and demand: all of a sudden there was such a glut of ancient Mesopotamian material that eventually prices fell, auction houses lost interest, collectors filled their boots and walked away.

It was, observed several journalists, 'the death of history'. The redoubtable Robert Fisk, suitably appalled and condemnatory, had recourse to the common (and lazy) metaphor about 'priceless' treasures. The truth was just the opposite: all this looting was occasioned by the fact that these objects *have* prices. There is an international market in them, though the on-site looters got only a tiny fraction of the prices in New York or London. As a report by local archaeologists (cited by Fisk) observed, looters 'have been trained in how to rob the world of its past and they have been making significant profit from it. They know the value of each object and it is difficult to see why they would stop looting.' Several of the looters, questioned as to why they wished to destroy historical sites of such 'priceless' value, simply replied that the nation had given them nothing, and cursed its history.

It was wicked, illegal and unseemly, and prompted furious discussion. In the West, the debate about Iraq's lost treasures centred on Chicago. In 2006 its Oriental Institute entitled an exhibition on the subject 'Catastrophe! The Looting and Destruction of Iraq's Past!' The institute took an unambiguous stance in opposition to the importation of stolen artefacts, and their purchase by international museums which 'actively encourage' donations from benefactors (who may receive a tax break in doing so) without questioning the provenance of the objects themselves. In contrast, the Institute announced proudly, they were vigilant about what they purchased or received as donations, lest they inadvertently encourage further theft and looting.

Seems clear enough, doesn't it? But the policy, or perhaps the self-congratulatory tone in which it was stated, prompted a provocative rejoinder from James Cumo, Director of The Art Institute of Chicago. According to Cumo, the question of who 'owns' antiquity is more complex than usually imagined. He is sceptical regarding the received wisdom that mere possession of the land on which antiquities are found entitles a present nation-state to claim them as its heritage. The argument, he feels, applies in our present case: 'Whatever it is,' he says, 'Iraqi national culture certainly doesn't include the antiquities of the region's Sumerian, Assyrian and Babylonian past.' Of course, he acknowledges, material stolen from the Baghdad Museum must be returned, but about the treasures previously taken from the archaeological sites he has his doubts. As his own museum's collection amply testifies, it is surely better for the artefacts to be properly housed abroad than left to lie in sites which are pillaged and damaged in casual ways.

Thus, to take a nice example: the Pergamon Museum in Berlin has as one of its finest attractions a reconstruction of the magnificent Babylonian Gate of Ishtar, dating from the sixth century BC, under the reign of King Nebuchadnezzar II, which are amongst my favourite relics of antiquity. The archaeological site from which it was long ago removed is, to this day, only partially excavated. Bits and pieces of the Gate can be found round the world, but only the Pergamon had the funds and imagination to put (some of it) back together again.

During the Iraq War, American military vehicles had levelled the original site to create helicopter landing areas and parking lots for tanks and other military vehicles. Twelve trenches were dug into the ancient deposits, still extant portions of the original Ishtar Gate were demolished, brick pavements more than 2,500 years old were crushed. Yet the Hague Convention and Protocol of 1954 prohibits the use of internationally recognised heritage sites for the installation of military bases. Many countries who sent forces to support the 'coalition' in Iraq were signatories to that treaty, including Australia, the Netherlands, Italy and Poland. The United States of America refused to sign.

No doubt these relics would have been safer and more widely enjoyed, if they were under Mr Cumo's care? Surely it is a mistake to assume that a putative home culture will take adequate care of its archaeological past?

We have a prize instance in our own British Museum. We are frequently told that it was an act of cultural vandalism when Lord Elgin removed many of the great marble friezes from the Parthenon in 1806, and carted them back from Athens to their eventual home in London. Apparently this was very bad of him. We are told this so often, and so heatedly, that it is now possible to mistake it for a received truth. To this day you will hardly find a Greek who doesn't believe they should be returned to Athens and reinstated at their original site.

But would the Marbles have survived the neglect of the nineteenth-century Athenians had Lord Elgin not seen fit to take them away? And he wasn't the only one: half of the Parthenon's sculptures are entirely lost, while various pieces are now in ten museums in eight different countries. For over a century the marble from the Parthenon had routinely been used as a source of building material, until the local Turks discovered, to their astonishment, that Western travellers would pay for bits of the sculptures. Did Lord Elgin save them for posterity, and ought his name to be honoured? Perhaps, I sometimes like to muse, the Parthenon ought to be transported to London to be reunited with its great friezes, in tacit acceptance of the fact that a homeland is not always the best place to preserve its own treasures. Perhaps it could be reassembled in Hyde Park and used as a drop-in centre for those disgraced Members of Parliament who faked their expense forms, and have lost both their jobs and their marbles.

This is frivolous, of course. But there is an ironic attendant gain that results from the multitudinous cultural transfers (if I may so designate them) which have for centuries filled museums with artefacts transported, often dubiously, from their original homelands. It is on the basis of such transfers that we are able, in country after country, to appreciate and to understand other cultures and to form, from childhood, lasting impressions of the richness and variety of other civilisations. The spooky embalmed cat at the British Museum, the Rosetta Stone, the Elgin Marbles were all features of my children's early education, and I am certain that, in however fugitive a manner, they developed differently and more richly than they would have done in the absence of such exposure. Were we without such opportunities – imagine museums which were severely limited to national artefacts – a profound source of pleasure and instruction would be lost. It is through such exposure that we can locate who we are, and how our culture differs from, contrasts to and overlaps with other cultures, both ancient and modern. Artefacts migrate in much the same way humans do, often with no discernible purpose or sense of destination, but when they put down roots they can enrich the community in which they settle.

If we embark upon a frenzy of giving back from one culture to another, we will come to have museums which are merely 'national', in which we cannot get adequate comparative glimpses of other pasts, where a kind of crimped provincialism holds sway, like those worthy but boring local museums that small towns use to illustrate and to explain their past.

It's a bit uncomfortable, finding myself in this paradoxical position, but it seems to me a little looting can go a long way. Has my inner Donald Rumsfeld begun to get the better of me? Civilisation may have begun in Mesopotamia, but it didn't stay there or end there. It is a now universal phenomenon, shared by the people of the world. There is much to rejoice in about this process, as well as much to regret.

It was one of the pleasures of having an office near the British Museum that there were antiquities dealers all around me. The shop opposite had astonishing treasures in its window: terracotta horses from China's Han period; Greek amphorae painted with scenes of war, the hunt or lustful pursuit; Roman glass beakers astonishingly intact after thousands of years; Persian bowls with beautiful designs in turquoise against a mushroom-coloured ground. I liked to watch people as they window-shopped, until they walked away, shaking their heads in bemusement at the prices. Too expensive? Quite the opposite. Nothing was priced at more than a couple of hundred pounds. They were, for objects of such high craftsmanship, beauty and antiquity, unimaginably cheap. The reason is simple: there are too many such treasures, their original homes having been stripped over centuries of hundreds of thousands of such objects.

Such treasures, I suspect, would be easier to sell at twenty times the price. But while they are still available, I buy them: as presents for my wife or for myself, and occasionally as wedding gifts, for I cannot bear offering a mass-produced ceramic bowl when I could give an antique Persian one. If the recipient is too young to appreciate such an object, surely they can grow into it? Such an object can open a world.

If there is anything, now, that might be called a cradle of civilisation, it is no longer Iraq. If you want to see the objects from such an archaeologically rich past, go to a museum. But even the British Museum, stuffed with relics of culture after culture, de-natures its holdings, sanitises and isolates them. In their original context such objects make sense, resonate with each other and with the landscapes in which they were generated. Stripped willy-nilly from those originating landscapes and cultural context, they take on a separate life of their own, become objects of contemplation and aesthetic value, like paintings. You strip a previously useful object of its utility and regard it purely for its form, as if it were intended as a work of art, as Marcel Duchamp wittily did in submitting a urinal – titled *Fountain* – to an art exhibition in 1917. Though it was never actually shown, and eventually lost, the point was clear: look at the thing in itself, wipe away the streams of urine and the object takes on an eerie attractiveness.

At the Pergamon Museum we are invited to view the great Gate of Ishtar as an object of contemplation, not of entry into a city; and though the available guides and headphones try to establish the original context, it is hard to imagine it. The Gate of Ishtar is the *Gate* of *Ishtar*, once one of the portals into a thriving city, grandly adorned but defined by their function; now it is merely (and wonderfully) a beautiful object in lapis lazuli with bas-relief auruchs and dragons. The Gates had a function and a place – were site-specific – and their utility and meaning can only be understood through their complex relations to the whole configuration not merely of that city but of Babylonian culture generally. But, of course, that is now quite impossible: bits and pieces of the original gates – the Pergamon reconstruction is of the eighth gate – are distributed in museums round the world: examples of bas-relief lions from other gates, for instance, may be found in museums in Boston, Chicago, Detroit, Gothenburg, Istanbul, Munich, New Haven, New York, Paris, Philadelphia and Toronto. The remnants of a great world city displayed in the great cities of the world.

This sounds all right: we are inured to it, and undeniably benefit from such cultural transmissions, however brutally achieved. But when we gawp appreciatively at the Mesopotamian and Sumerian artefacts in the museums to which they have been transported, it is impossible not to recognise, too, how much has been lost, in converting material that had a living presence in an ancient culture into isolated works of art in an exhibition hall: beautiful and inspiring, to be sure, but detached and denatured, ironically stripped of meaning in the very act of demonstrating how very meaningful they once were.

14

The Savaging of Africa:
The Sacking of the Lost Kingdom of Benin

It is one of the most memorable images of the American 1960s, a decade notable for its unforgettable visual records: of the assassinations of the Kennedy brothers and Martin Luther King, student riots and political protests, demonstrations against the atrocities of the Vietnam War. Yet even in the midst of this compelling turmoil I can still recall vividly the image of three Olympic athletes standing on the rostrum to receive their medals after the 200 metre sprint, in which Tommie Smith had just set a new world record of 19.83 seconds. Time for that simple joyous celebration and pride which Olympic winners demonstrate, tears rolling down their cheeks as their national anthem echoes tinnily through the stadium? Not for a hundredth of a second.

As the Star Spangled Banner played – *the land of the free and the home of the brave!* – both Tommie Smith and John Carlos, who won the bronze, bowed their heads as each lifted his arm, black-gloved fist clenched, in the Black Power salute that had mobilised a new generation of angry young people into opposition to the endemic racism of American culture. It was a thrilling moment, totally unexpected, of breath-taking simplicity and nobility. To make it even more shocking and powerful, they were joined in their protest by the silver medal winner, the Australian Peter Norman, who did not raise his arm but, like the others, was wearing the badge of the Olympic Project for Human Rights, in support of Australia's Aboriginals.

Olympic Project for *Human Rights*? Seems some sort of oxymoron. The project was certainly *not* generated by the organisers of the Games themselves, but was the brainchild of the sociologist Harry Edwards, who had urged a boycott of the Games by blacks, and whose ideas had apparently catalysed the protest by the three athletes. It was an extraordinarily imaginative and courageous gesture in the Olympic context, unprecedented. The two Americans were both vilified and applauded, but it was impossible to deny the power and authority of what they had done.

Olympic athletes do not protest. They not only capitulate to the crass nationalism of the Games, they embrace it. Though they are, supremely, individual athletes in search of individual glory, they enfold themselves in the phoney nationalist ethos of the Games. After being booed off the podium, Smith put this baldly: 'If I win, I am American, not a black American. But if I did something bad, then they would say I am a Negro. We are black and we are proud of being black. Black America will understand what we did tonight.' Smith and Carlos were suspended from the United States team and ordered to leave the Olympic Village. Avery Brundage, the creepy, reactionary President of the International Olympic Committee, announced that sport and politics must be entirely separate.

A bronze from the Kingdom of Benin, looted by British soldiers in 1897. As recently as 1972 original Benin bronzes were being sold by the British Museum.

This happened in October 1968, the year that also saw the publication of Eldridge Cleaver's *Soul on Ice*. Written in Folsom prison, this former dope dealer and 'insurrectionary rapist' was a follower of Malcolm X (whose own *Autobiography* was published in 1965). Both advocated a breakaway from America's racist culture and promoted the fantasy of some sort of return, whether literal or spiritual, to Africa. Black Americans, first classed as Negroes, then as coloureds, more recently as blacks, were, now, none of the above: they were African-Americans. It was hard, for a time, to keep up with the approved nomenclature.

Africa, properly understood, was a homeland to be proud of, the history of which had been whitewashed and rewritten by European and American colonialists. Malcolm X puts the point concisely:

> But if you want to take the time to do research for yourself, I think you'll find that on the African continent there was always, prior to the discovery of America, there was always a higher level of history, rather a higher level of culture and civilization, than that which existed in Europe at the same time.

Of course, this claim knowingly and misleadingly conflates Saharan with sub-Saharan Africa, and presumably rests much of its case on the achievements of the Islamic cultures of the north, whereas Malcolm X's real constituency was of those sub-Saharans who had become slaves, captured and often transported – this is worse than ironic – by North African, Arab slavers. But Malcolm X (a follower of Elijah Muhammad, as Cassius Clay was to become as well) had joined the Nation of Islam, and was doctrinally inclined to treat Africa as if it were a single entity. The followers of this movement were curiously unengaged with the loathsome practices of the Arab slave traders.

Nevertheless, I read both Malcolm X and Cleaver with fascinated respect, and if I knew little about African-American life, and less about Africa, it was impossible to deny the justice of their case and the righteousness of the anger that Smith and Carlos so perfectly symbolised on the Olympic rostrum.

At exactly that time – the autumn of 1968 – I began work on my Oxford D.Phil. thesis on Joseph Conrad. My focus was on what I called 'The Moral World of the Novelist', in which I tried to trace the uneasy relations, in his work, between a cosmology which insists on the ultimate meaningless of things and that traditional Conradian imperative for personal responsibility, upright conduct – 'honour' – which is based so firmly on the principles that govern life – or should govern life – amongst the crew of a ship.

I read the fiction chronologically, tracing the development of this theme, so it was hardly any time before I came to consider the first of Conrad's works to be set in Africa, *Heart of Darkness*, the most remarkable evocation of that continent from that period, and of its haunting pull on the minds of the Europeans who went there. Mr Kurtz, the subject of the tale, finds that his deeply civilised nature – 'all Europe went into the making of him' – is inadequate to resist a regression into 'savage' and unspeakable practices (head-hunting and cannibalism are suggested). He has honoured the natives with his presence, and been undermined by theirs. In Africa he encounters what that great Nigerian writer Chinua Achebe later described as an 'unconscious primeval hegemony that had apparently gone nowhere and seen nobody since the world was created'.

Mr Kurtz's final words are a judgement of the adventures of his soul upon this earth, but also a howl of regret for the pleasures of an unrestrained godhead abandoned. 'The horror! The horror!' is a judgement made by the Ego upon the Id. Conrad's narrator, Marlow, is duly and rightly horrified, and wise enough, on a later encounter with Mr Kurtz's fiancée, to lie to her and to claim that Kurtz's last words were 'your name'. Through such lies is the darkness held uneasily at bay, that civilisation may protect its thin veneer.

Africans may have been 'savages' to Marlow, but they were also – marginally if recognisably – human beings. As his boat drifts down the Congo, it is greeted by an incomprehensible cacophony, deafening and terrifying, from the jungle along the banks:

> The prehistoric man was cursing us, praying to us, welcoming us – who could tell? … we glided past like phantoms, wondering and secretly appalled, as sane men would before an enthusiastic outbreak in a madhouse. We could not understand … because we were travelling in the night of first ages … It was unearthly, and the men were – No, they were not inhuman. Well, you know that was the worst of it – this suspicion of their not being inhuman … what thrilled you was just the thought of their humanity – like yours – the thought of your remote kinship with this wild and passionate uproar.

In a seminal essay on racism in *Heart of Darkness* (an

'offensive and deplorable book') published in 1977, Achebe quotes from this passage, and is appalled. This supposedly enlightened thinking is mere verbiage, and the tortuous double negative ('not … inhuman') itself seems to indicate some unease in the telling, though it may have some slight mitigating value. But the sentiment places Marlow in a tradition of European visitors who have, in Achebe's words, encountered in Africa 'the antithesis of Europe and therefore of civilization, a place where man's vaunted intelligence and refinement are finally mocked by triumphant bestiality'.

Even Conrad, who tried to distinguish between bad colonialists (Belgians, Portuguese) and better ones (British), and who was unrelenting in his condemnation of the greedy exploitation of Africa by rapacious and cruel Europeans, nevertheless felt that the subjugated peoples in these countries were, *au fond*, alike. Similarly simple, primitive, emotionally unreliable, warlike and childlike: in need of firm restraint, and the sort of guidance imposed from without.

Thus we have Marlow's patronising respect for an African who has been trained to do a simple repetitive job:

And between whiles I had to look after the savage who was fireman. He was an improved specimen; he could fire up a vertical boiler. He was there below me and, upon my word, to look at him was as edifying as seeing a dog in a parody of breeches and a feather hat walking on his hind legs. A few months of training had done for that really fine chap. He squinted at the steam-gauge and at the water-gauge with an evident effort of intrepidity – and he had filed his teeth too, the poor devil, and the wool of his pate shaved into queer patterns, and three ornamental scars on each of his cheeks. He ought to have been clapping his hands and stamping his feet on the bank, instead of which he was hard at work, a thrall to strange witchcraft, full of improving knowledge.

If you are not embarrassed reading his passage, you should be. In the old days – when I was writing that D.Phil. – Conradians were *not*, though many are now, as a succeeding generation of post-colonial critics has taken up Achebe's challenge: 'His obvious racism has, however, not been addressed. And it is high time it was!'

For Conrad, the choice for an African was simple: either learn the fireman's trade or remain a savage, unrestrained and virtually unrestrainable. Presumably unlike Europeans, who are capable of slaughter on a scale undreamt of by the hungriest cannibal or most acquisitive collector of heads. Perhaps we need to recall Gulliver's enthusiastic account, to his Houyhnhnm friend, of the European 'art of war':

I gave him a description of cannons, culverins, muskets, carbines, pistols, bullets, powder, swords, bayonets, battles, sieges, retreats, attacks, undermines, countermines, bombardments, sea fights, ships sunk with a thousand men, twenty thousand killed on each side, dying groans, limbs flying in the air, smoke, noise, confusion, trampling to death under horses' feet, flight, pursuit, victory; fields strewed with carcases, left for food to dogs and wolves and birds of prey; plundering, stripping, ravishing, burning, and destroying. And to set forth the valour of my own dear countrymen, I assured him, that I had seen them blow up a hundred enemies at once in a siege, and as many in a ship, and beheld the dead bodies drop down in pieces from the clouds, to the great diversion of the spectators.

Entranced by this glorious spectacle, Gulliver is eventually hushed by his master's horrified response that 'whoever understood the nature of *Yahoos,* might easily believe it possible for so vile an animal to be capable of every action I had named.' That is – surely it is clear enough by now? – there are plenty of savages about. They are called humans.

It should have been no great surprise, then, that those who came from without to impose such restraint might well have lacked it themselves, like Conrad's Mister Kurtz. The benefits of civilisation are tenuous, and the atavistic appeal of 'savage' regression needed constantly to be resisted. Africa was, for Conrad's generation, a testing place for the strength of one's moral fibre. It was the 'dark' continent, the blackness of its peoples a manifestation of lack. This was a useful belief if you were intent on plunder, whether under the guise of benevolent colonial development or simply for individual self-enrichment.

A belief in the innate savagery of the African, and his pressing need for betterment, was also held by the ostensibly benevolent, indeed often relatively enlightened, group of missionaries, explorers, adventurers and colonialists who were compulsive and numerous visitors in the nineteenth and twentieth centuries. These 'friends' of Africa often shared Albert Schweitzer's patronising dictum: 'The African is indeed my brother but my junior brother.' Not *younger*, but junior, which is to say no brother at all.

It takes little thought or investigation to see that this attitude to Africa is, still, common enough, and that many prevailing contemporary images of that continent continue to partake of such dismissiveness. References to Africans as 'Third-World' often carry implicit claims of primitivism; condemnations of bloodthirsty dictators and potentates replace claims of tribal savagery. Though a generation of post-colonial scholarship has effectively placed and dismissed such stereotypes, they are curiously adhesive in the public imagination.

What intrigues and embarrasses me, in retrospect, is how two of the dominant strains of my life in Oxford working on my D.Phil. should have had so little contact with each other. I hugely admired, and was moved *both* by Tommie Smith's Black Power salute and by Conrad's enlightened belief in the kinship, if you were 'man enough' to acknowledge it, between the light and the dark, the civilised and the savage, the European and the African. That the implications of the Black Power and black pride movement were damaging to Conrad's view never occurred to me, and when I now reread my commentary on *Heart of Darkness*, I see that I never mentioned, because I did not recognise, the dehumanising effect of its treatment of its Africans.

I was hardly alone in this blindness and ignorance, for if you consult the available commentaries on Conrad produced in the '60s and '70s, none mentions what now seems obvious: that there is something blankly Eurocentric and worse than patronising about Conrad's view of the dark continent and its peoples. For Conrad, Africa was as it ever has been. *Where, after all, was the evidence to the contrary?* If Africans were to be accorded the rights and respect offered from the peoples of one civilisation to another, what could you point to by way of their achievements?

Picasso's appropriation of 'primitive' art had suggested that, if you had a sufficiently creative eye, you might see beauty where others saw only crude fetish objects. Yes, seen through the right pair of eyes, Africans could carve objects of considerable power and beauty. The art historian Frank Willett notes that it was

> in 1904–5 that African art began to make its distinctive impact. One piece is still identifiable; it is a mask that had been given to Maurice Vlaminck in 1905. He records that Derain was 'speechless' and 'stunned' when he saw it, bought it from Vlaminck and in turn showed it to Picasso and Matisse, who were also greatly affected by it. Ambroise Vollard then borrowed it and had it cast in bronze ... The revolution of twentieth-century art was under way!

It is particularly pleasing that the mask was Congolese, from the Fang people whom Marlow – and Conrad! – might have encountered, without pausing to look, on that trip down the river.

The revolutionary effect of Picasso's *Demoiselles d'Avignon* in 1907 was based in large part not on its fragmented pre-Cubist perspective but on the tribal mask-like faces with which the *femmes de nuit* were adorned, bringing with them not merely a reminder of the ostensibly savage and unrestrained but also – shockingly – the implicit suggestion that such artefacts might be assimilated into the regions of European high art.

It didn't take long for the European artistic respect for

the newly discovered art of sub-Saharan Africa to reach the conservative shores of England. In D. H. Lawrence's *Women in Love* (1921) Rupert Birkin and Gerald Crich are studying an African 'fetish' sculpture of a woman in labour.

'Why is it art?' Gerald asked, shocked, resentful.
'It conveys a complete truth,' said Birkin. 'It contains the whole truth of that state, whatever you feel about it.'
'But you can't call it *high* art,' said Gerald.
'High! There are centuries and hundreds of centuries of development in a straight line, behind that carving; it is an awful pitch of culture, of a definite sort.'

This sounds good, a genuinely fresh act of perception on Birkin's part – that is, until he takes it all back.

'What culture?' Gerald asked, in opposition. He hated the sheer African thing.
'Pure culture in sensation, culture in the physical consciousness, really ultimate *physical* consciousness, mindless, utterly sensual. It is so sensual as to be final, supreme.'

The fetish is art of a *primitive* kind, mindless, sunk in the experience of the body and (even worse) 'the blood'. If it is not inferior to the art of civilised societies, which represents the life of the mind, it is radically different from it. If art at all, it is the art of savages.

Are objects like this 'fetish' merely recovered cultural artefacts, giving us a window into a foreign form of life, or are they – also – rightly to be regarded as works of art? There is, clearly, a category problem here, and the curators

233

of the British Museum had had it as well. The present-day explanatory note to the Benin exhibition acknowledges the problem, and multiplies it: if the objects were worthy of the label 'art', then how was it possible that the ancient Beninese had created them? Benin brasswork, we are reminded, 'so confounded current ideas about Africa that some refused to believe that it could be of exclusively Benin origin'.

In any case, if you scanned the African landscapes for further examples of artistic achievement, what would you find? The literary heritage, such as it was, was largely oral. There were no obvious instances of sophisticated architecture, painting or sculpture, or of striking social integration across tribes rather than within them. There was nothing to compare with the great achievements of North Africa. No civilisation.

To the conventional nineteenth-century European mind – indeed, to many minds today – there was a clear discrimination between the cultures of North Africa (Egypt, Libya, Morocco, Tunisia), in which the residue of Graeco-Roman antiquity still echoed, and the great vitality of high Islamic culture and architecture was still visible. But, south of the Sahara – in the 'real' Africa – what might one say about that? What was there to see?

Quite a lot, in fact, but it largely goes unsaid and unseen. The British Museum, that great repository of the art and architecture of the rest of the world, has a significant holding of objects, many of them on display for generations, which testify to a quality of art and culture in sub-Saharan Africa which men of the stature of David Livingstone and Conrad had either failed to notice, or to appreciate. Evidence aplenty that 'Africa' had always been a land of 'civilisation' in exactly the sense that Conrad had denied. Why didn't he know this? Or – more appropriately – why don't most of us?

Here is a nice bit of synchronicity: at much the same time that Conrad was beginning to write *Heart of Darkness*, an unauthorised British expeditionary force entered the kingdom of Benin, ostensibly to enforce an 1892 'treaty of friendship' (known as the Gallwey Treaty) that King Omo n'Oba Ovonramwen had rightly refused to sign. He recognised that, beneath the usual rhetoric, it would have made his lands into a British 'Protectorate', as such were often, and ironically, labelled. Rightly alarmed, the king banned British visitors to his kingdom, rightly fearing their intentions, for the unreciprocated offer of 'friendship' had become, in British eyes, an excuse for an invasion of Benin.

Late in 1896 an invading force led by Lieutenant James Phillips, which consisted of six British officers and some 250 African soldiers, set out to capture the city of Benin, depose its king and lay hold of its many assets. On learning that the force was on its way, the king was inclined to let them into the city to declare their intentions, but was overruled by the commander of his army, whose pre-emptive strike against the would-be invaders killed most of the soldiers and all but two of the British officers. It was a terrible slaughter – the so-called force was totally unprepared for the attack – and feelings in London were incendiary. Benin must be taught a lesson.

What the British reprisal soon did, aside from killing a great many Beninese, was not merely to destroy the remnants of a great and ancient culture but to strip its artistic assets – (in order to 'defray the cost of the war') – including over 900 of those magnificent bronzes that were for centuries produced there, and which are now the property of museums throughout the world, particularly in Germany and at the University of Pennsylvania, with a few left for the British Museum.

The British had had their eye on the kingdom of Benin for some time. It was a stable and complex civilisation dating back to the tenth century, with records of some thirty-one kings, itself a crisp rejoinder to Oxford Professor Hugh Trevor-Roper's assertion that there was 'no such thing' as African history. Indeed, Europeans had been visiting Benin for centuries, and came back mightily impressed by the culture that they encountered. Olfert Dapper, a seventeenth-century Dutch traveller, gave an enthusiastic account of his travels:

> The King's court is certainly as large as the town of Haarlem, and is entirely surrounded by a special wall … It is divided into many magnificent palaces, houses, and apartments of the courtiers. Fine galleries, about as large as those on the Exchange at Amsterdam, are supported by wooden pillars, from top to bottom covered with cast copper on which are engraved the pictures of their war exploits and battles, and they are kept very clean.

Benin City continued to thrive, and its earthwork fortifications were the second-largest man-made structure in the world, after the Great Wall of China. With streets 130 feet wide, it had been a major centre of trade and craft for many centuries. It was a relatively safe compound, protected by some nine ornate gates, themselves works of art comparable in quality to those of the city of the goddess Ishtar. The palace, the major building within the city, was an enormous structure of some 2 million square feet. Very little of this remains. The British force of 1897 destroyed most of the city walls, though some remnants can still be seen today.

The Benin bronzes taken after the 1897 raid were (finally) acknowledged as 'booty' in an in-house British Museum report of 1972, which nevertheless insisted there was nothing illegal about their acquisition. It was just a little unseemly, perhaps? The history of the bronzes since the Museum acquired 203 plaques from the Home Office in 1898 is an object lesson in how complex the problem of 'acquiring' other cultures' works of art can be, and how difficult it is to frame consistent and morally justifiable policies with regard to their display, storage and possible de-accessioning.

In 1950, some thirty of the plaques were described as 'duplicate specimens' by the Keeper of Ethnography, who proposed that they be sold back to Nigeria, which was contemplating establishing a museum in Lagos, and was naturally anxious to acquire some examples of its own treasures. A sale of ten plaques for £150 was agreed.

The Nigerians were keen to buy more examples, but two problems now arose. First, it was hard to tell how much the bronzes were worth, since few had been sold on the open market. (The solution was to appoint a dealer, operating on commission, to see what prices could be obtained.) But the second problem made a solution to the first increasingly unnecessary. What counts, other curators and officials began to demand, as a 'duplicate specimen'? The answer was shocking. A 'duplicate' showed the same sort of figures, but not necessarily in the same configuration. Thus an image of a king was held to duplicate any other image of a king. (Why not sell off 'duplicate' Rembrandt portraits of men, because, after all, he did lots of them?) It was a remarkably stupid policy, made even more astonishing when it was acknowledged that identical wall plaques were often hung in pairs, on either side of the entrance to the King's Palace. In selling one, their original purpose was lost.

Throughout the 1950s the British Museum continued to sell off occasional plaques, many of them to the Nigerians, in a series of transactions that, viewed in retrospect, seem haphazard and unaccompanied by any clear set of policy goals. The British Museum Act of 1963 attempted to impose some sort of order on these chaotic procedures, but an occasional sale of the bronzes was made until 1972. But if the policy was lax, the aims of the de-accessioning were frequently benign, being an attempt to bolster the holdings in Nigeria, which had become independent in 1960. Prices were set at reasonable levels, but none was simply repatriated in acknowledgment of its questionable status. It would have been hard to justify doing so, because if one plaque is returned without charge, why not all of them?

Anyway, one thing was clear: even with occasional de-accessioning, the Benin bronzes were a lot safer, and more accessible, in their home in London than they were in Lagos.

If you wish to study the civilisation and art of Benin, there is little sense going there. Go to a museum, a Western museum, instead. Go, perhaps, to the University of Pennsylvania, where Richard Hodges, the Director of the Penn Museum, notes proudly that some 20,000 important African objects may be found, including what is undoubtedly one of the finest collections of Benin art in the world. Writing about the 'Imagine Africa at the Penn Museum' exhibition, he observed: 'The question is – how do we make that collection, and our presentation of it, relevant to today's visitors, and particularly to the African and African American communities we serve in the region today?'

It is impossible not to observe, in response to this, that you only need to 'imagine Africa' because places like the Penn Museum house artefacts appropriated from that continent. If they were still there – and those hundreds of thousands of other such objects distributed round the world – could Conrad and his like have really maintained that Africans were 'savages?' We only need to 'imagine' Africa, the civilisations of Africa, because so many of the original sites have been rendered unimaginable, because it has been stripped of its cultural and artistic heritage so efficiently that it might never have been there at all. Indeed, to explorers, missionaries, colonialists, ivory hunters and traders – and the occasional novelist – it was not. No, it was one of the 'dark' places of the earth.

Consider how different it would be, to be a contemporary Nigerian, if there was a national museum of magnificent national objects in Lagos. (There is such a holding, but it is relatively modest in scope and presentation, and its administrators are constantly requesting the repatriation of their looted objects.) Heritage is not merely history, nor can it be located in some simple way in objects. A culture, its values and beliefs, is introjected. It becomes a formative part of who we are. Perhaps young Nigerians might define themselves and their culture that little bit differently, were such splendours available to admire and to study. Hardly the descendants of savages, but the inheritors of a once sophisticated and artistically literate civilisation. If you want to confirm this, go to Philadelphia, New York, London or Berlin. Most of what you will find in Nigeria is tacky airport art, based roughly on the original artefacts.

In what ways are the rights of man and the rights of nations to be compared? The transmission of cultural objects as the spoils of war is an essential part of the diaspora of objects of art, and is regarded as inalienable. But it is hard to justify the looting of the Benin bronzes even in this mitigated if conventional sense. Britain was not at war with the kingdom of Benin, and its first, unauthorised, attempt to sack the city was punished with a justified pre-emptive strike. British reprisals were fierce, and totally out of scale with the moral imperatives, and it is hard to see why Nigeria should not regard the restitution of the bronzes as their moral and legal right. The friezes and columns of the Parthenon had fallen into ruin, and were regularly stripped, even by locals, not for their artistic value but to use as building material. The Egyptians left the treasures of the kingdom to crumble in the desert air. The Oba, on the other hand, had enhanced and protected their treasures.

Nor was the destruction of the kingdom of Benin an isolated incident. Those most respected of Conrad's colonialists, the British, were also responsible, at much the same time as the sacking of Benin City, for destroying Kumasi, the capital of the Ashante empire, which was located in what is now called Ghana. For some hundreds of years a prosperous centre of trade and agriculture hacked out of the indigenous forest, the Ashante thrived due to the huge reserves of gold, and a relatively enlightened importation of slave labour. At its height, Kumasi had a population of some 2 million people, and was a thriving urban culture with a grand palace for the king, and a plethora of art works and jewellery fashioned from gold. The Ashante were literate, and the palace, according to one traveller, had a great many books, as well as sophisticated systems of law and trading.

Britain had been in armed conflict with the Ashante four times in the nineteenth century, drawn by the vast wealth, natural resources and trading power of the kingdom. Repulsed respectively in 1823 and 1863, a protracted assault on Kumasi in 1873–4 lead to a Treaty of Peace on terms favourable to the British, and to the sacking by some 2,500 soldiers of large parts of the city, and the destruction of the Royal Palace. In 1902, to no one's surprise, the land became a British Protectorate, and was renamed the Gold Coast.

This is only one of many such stories of cultural destruction. In fact, there were a widespread and thriving set of urban cultures in sub-Saharan Africa, sometimes with a strong Islamic influence and at other times not, for centuries before the European colonial development. Some of these cities, located in southern Africa, were built not with the usual mud, timber and thatch but had major stone edifices. A member of the London Missionary Society expedition of 1829 reported that, on his visits to the Orange River, he had encountered the ruins of large numbers of towns and cities, some 'of amazing extent', with clear evidence of 'immense labour and perseverance, every fence being composed of stones … raised without mortar, lime or hammer [and] examples of high-quality plastering, with cornicing and architraves, survive, and highly polished walls of the ruins of the houses still gleam from their original finish.'

Such remnants are, of course, testimony not to a thriving 'African' civilisation – there is no such thing – but to many, often competing, urban centres spread round the continent. You do not need to claim that these were the rivals of Venice to conclude that anyone who thinks, with Professor Trevor-Roper, that there is no such thing as African history or culture, is damagingly ignorant. This ignorance, though, is understandable, and is to this day widespread. When you survey most contemporary cities of sub-Saharan Africa, they are largely the residue of colonialism, and the conclusion that this is all there is, or ever has been, is too easily drawn.

Cultures, civilisations, cities, magnificent edifices come and go. We know that. The present state of Iraq has only minimal surviving testimony to the grandeur of the civilisations that have inhabited those lands. But we do not regard the Iraqis as savages, and we continue to regard ancient Mesopotamia with the highest respect.

Yet we have no such regard for Africa, or for its many lost civilisations. This was the fault not merely of widespread warring between tribal factions – cultures destroy themselves and each other – but is more substantially the legacy of colonialism. It is due to rapacity, to disrespect, to greed and to blindness. It is the fault of myriad visitors to the 'dark continent' in the nineteenth century, the well-intentioned as well as the merely venal. Sometimes it is hard to tell them apart.

But it is the fault, too, sadly and demonstrably, of the most brilliant and acute chroniclers of this spectacle. Of Joseph Conrad. And of ourselves, unconsciously accepting the prevailing myths, unwilling to look, and to revise our received images, and to learn. To learn, as Tommie Smith and John Carlos demonstrated, that there is so much to be proud of in this heritage, and so much to be angry about as a result of its loss.

15

Born to Blush Unseen: The Lost Buildings of Charles Rennie Mackintosh

I have spent some time recently – too much time, it's rather addictive – tucked away in my garden shed ogling a naughty magazine that I buy at my local newsagent, who sells it quite unashamedly to a coterie of lustful consumers. I'm embarrassed to admit it, but I can hardly put it down. It's full of gorgeous full-frontal pictures, though the private bits are discreetly hidden away. There are some nice rear views as well.

There's no need to be censorious. You may well buy it too. It's called *Country Life,* which is to the fantasies of the English middle classes what *Playboy* was to the young men of my own generation. The magazine is largely purchased – as *Playboy* was – by people who want to drool over the pictures, not to read the articles. It responds to our desire, and enhances it: it is architectural pornography.

The English – professional city people – lust after country residences as a tangible sign of success; in class terms a substantial country house allows the illusion of joining a rural squirearchy. You make your pile, and then you buy one: pick out something just right in a fashionable county, take up country pursuits, chop wood, plan a kitchen garden, go to school fairs, patronise the local farmer and the vicar, hunt a little perhaps, invite envious friends for the weekend.

The good life? Americans never consider even the possibility: a summer month in Maine or the Hamptons is perfectly adequate by way of rural exposure. And the French, with typical perversity, do just the opposite to *les Anglais*. No sooner have they inherited a *grande maison* or château in idyllic surroundings than they have sold it to an English couple. *So cheap darling! And so pretty!*

But there is a downside to this château-coveting, Georgian-rectory chasing middle-class fantasy: English people do not dream of designing and building a new house. Almost never. Indeed, the very term 'architecturally designed' has become so debased that it now means *not* architecturally designed, not individual, not an enactment of an individual client's individual dreams. It's a branding phrase used by mega-builders of pseudo-swish flats and housing developments.

Yes, land is expensive, it is hard to find the right plot and architect, planning permission can be a nightmare, you will struggle to control costs – these and a thousand other fears and caveats deter the few possible brave souls who wish to build something uniquely their own. It's been this way for a while. There were a few Edwardians who commissioned (say) Edwin Lutyens to build something grand, personal and amusing. But for every Lutyens, there were dozens of capable architects without sufficient customers to keep them afloat.

Even, and this is deeply shocking, even Charles Rennie Mackintosh, the most brilliant British architect of the twentieth century, couldn't find enough customers to sustain an

Born to blush unseen: Mackintosh's design for Liverpool Cathedral (1903).

architectural practice. Born in Glasgow in 1868, this preter-
naturally talented young man studied at the Glasgow School
of Art, and was already a partner in an architectural firm by
the age of twenty-three. It was an ideal time to be working:
Glasgow, known as the second city of empire, was expand-
ing massively: railway stations, hotels, municipal buildings,
factories, urban housing developments and individual villas
were all necessary, and a virtual renaissance in the arts
accompanied the commercial boom.

Omnivorously inquisitive, Mackintosh developed at an
astonishing rate. He won scholarships for overseas study
and travel, gorged himself on the new architectural journals, studied Japanese architecture and style. Mackintosh
had a rage for design, and became as well known for his
furniture, fabrics, graphics, cutlery, light fixtures and wall
decorations as for his (relatively few) buildings. His chairs,
for instance, are instantly recognisable, objects of surpassing
attractiveness, as long as you don't try to sit in them.

Of his early work, the Glasgow School of Art, which he
designed in his late twenties, is undoubtedly his masterpiece, and its north façade has been described by that great
American architect Robert Venturi as 'one of the greatest
achievements of all time, comparable in scale and majesty to
Michelangelo'. It is a remarkable claim, made more fascinating by the fact that Mackintosh had so skilfully outstripped
his brief ('Tis but a plain building that is desired') and the
crimped budget that accompanied it. The result of his
labour now makes one catch one's breath in astonishment
and admiration, but at the time the building went largely
unregarded. The governors of the School of Art congratu-
lated themselves on having commissioned and produced

(no mention is made of the architect) a 'sound, substantial workmanlike building'.

Perhaps this response, in some cock-eyed way, is a sort of compliment. To the ignorant eye the building may have looked like a competent pastiche of Scottish baronial and vernacular styles, for Mackintosh had managed to combine many fresh and modern elements that were still subsumed in the overall look. Yet it was not only the purblind administrators who could not see what was so triumphantly before their eyes; most of the architectural establishment couldn't either. The building went virtually unrecognised in the Scottish and English press, and only the art journal *The Studio* (which published photographs of a few of the interiors) gave it any serious consideration. Yet on the continent the building was widely recognised as a work of genius.

If the first stage of the School of Art was recognisably and untroublingly Scottish, the subsequent building phase ten years later was in a more modern style, light and airy, the interiors fresh and inventive. The library, completed in 1909, was based on Japanese models, with a delightful use of beams and timbers, and is the undoubted highlight of the building. Though this extraordinary achievement led to a few further commissions, of which Hill House for the publisher Walter Blackie, and the charming tea rooms for his patron Miss Cranston are the finest, it did not, sadly, herald the beginning of a sustained architectural practice.

Mackintosh is probably most widely recognised as a designer of Glasgow tea rooms, which sounds modest enough but wasn't. In the eighteenth century coffee houses were the usual meeting places in London, but by the 1840s they had been replaced by tea houses, as the drinking of tea became the norm in English culture. In London, Twining's had been the first of the tea houses, but it was overtaken by Lyons Tea Rooms, which from the 1890s were the meeting place of choice. The Lyons Corner Houses in the West End were capacious establishments, often on four or five floors of an elegant building, offering both meals and a counter service, as well as telephone booths, ticket-purchasing kiosks and hair-dressing salons (which reflected the largely female clientele).

In Glasgow the tea house was also to become a fashionable upmarket establishment, a trend initiated in 1878 by Kate Cranston, or 'Miss Cranston' as she was known, whose empire grew substantially over the next thirty years. An eccentric, strong-willed businesswoman, she was an immediately recognisable Glasgow figure, with her taste for homemade dresses that swirled and flounced dramatically, rather wonderful hats, and imperious manner. Her brother had preceded her in the tea business and opened tea rooms before her, but he had neither her drive nor her extraordinary conviction that a tea house could become the very centre of Glasgow life.

She had an uncommon combination of intelligence, good taste and commercial acumen, at a time when women rarely opened their own businesses, and even less commonly succeeded when they did so. So certain was Miss Cranston that she would be shunned not merely by polite society but by her own friends and family, that she paid what she called 'going-away' calls on them, 'because they would not want to know her when she had become a businesswoman'.

But before very long, they did. Everybody did. It was virtually impossible to live a full and happy life in Glasgow and not visit Miss Cranston's Tea Rooms. From the beginning she believed that if the venture was going to succeed, the tea rooms (unlike those in London) would have to attract men. Ladies were easy, the natural constituency of such premises, but what would draw a male clientele? The answer was a mixture of men-only rooms (including smoking and billiard rooms) with their own 'masculine' decorations and furnishings – 'dark and solid' – and a menu that included the kind of old-fashioned fare, such as pie and chips, that could be found in local pubs (and at much the same price). The fact that Miss Cranston's, unlike those pubs, did not serve beer or spirits, was turned shrewdly to her advantage, for there was too much drunkenness in Glasgow, and wives were certain to encourage their menfolk's entry into this salubrious, but dry, environment.

She had the confidence and money to indulge her taste, and was to become Mackintosh's major patron for over twenty years. She first employed him and his capable wife ('Margaret has genius, I only have talent') in 1897 – the same year in which he began working on designs for the Glasgow School of Art – to do many of the interior designs for the walls on three floors, with murals, stencilling and decorations, of her Buchanan Street Tea Rooms. The effect (colours were subtly modulated from 'greyish-greenish yellow' upwards to blue as you rose through the building, as if from earth to sky) was delightful, startlingly new, totally arresting. For only 2d. one could have a cup of tea and enter a set of rooms that were, themselves, fully integrated works of art.

Miss Cranston's new rooms were almost immediately designated as must-sees for any tourist to Glasgow, and one such was Edwin Lutyens, anxious to observe what all the fuss was about:

> a Miss Somebody's who is really a Mrs Somebody else. She has started a large Restaurant, all very elaborately simple on very new school High Arts Lines. The result is gorgeous! And a wee bit vulgar! She has nothing but green-handled knives and all is curiously painted and coloured … Some of the knives are purple and are put as spots of colour! It is all quite good, all just a little *outré*, a thing we must avoid and shall too.

Anyone who does not detect the sound of envy amidst this mitigated enthusiasm isn't listening very hard. (Within a few years green-handled knives were used in the Lutyens household, and he brought home with him from Glasgow a basketful of Miss Cranston's 'most delicious' blue-willow pattern china.)

Mackintosh's major contribution to Miss Cranston's burgeoning empire, in which he had total control of the project from the refurbishment of a modest tenement building to the interior designs and furnishing, was the Willow Tea Rooms, which opened in 1903. According to Perilla Kinchin, whose *Taking Tea with Mackintosh* is the best guide to the relationship, a contemporary photograph of the Salon de Luxe shows:

> eight high-backed silver chairs, decorated with oval cut-outs and squares of purple glass, carefully lined up at the central tables on the marked-out carpet. At the side of the room are chairs with lower curved backs, also silver, and

upholstered in purple velvet. The lower walls were pan-
elled with silvery purple silk, stitched with beads down
the seams. Margaret had contributed a decorative panel
in gesso, her favourite medium: three elongated ladies,
dripping with strings of glass jewels ... Above was a chan-
delier of countless pink glass baubles ... Round the walls
ran a frieze of leaded coloured and mirror glass, reflecting and refracting the customers of this fantasy world.

The spirit and aesthetic of the Vienna Secession is apparent, for Mackintosh was not only revered in Europe but had
derived many of his ideas from continental models. Glaswe-
gians flocked to the new rooms, and even the intimidated
working classes made their wary way into this splendid
setting. The journalist Neil Munro, who wrote the popular
'Erchie' column in the *Evening News,* had some fun with the
notion of introducing two unsophisticated working men
into this middle-class paradise, and suggesting they tuck
into the cakes:

> It was a real divert. It was the first time ever he had a knife
> and fork to eat cookies wi', and he thocht his teaspoon was
> a' bashed oot o' its richt shape till I tellt him whit that was
> whit made it Art. 'Art,' says he, 'whit the mischief's Art.'

But they do not stay for too long, because Mackintosh's
chairs not only had a tendency to wobble and eventually
to fall apart, but were also distinctly uncomfortable to sit
in, or on. This apparent failing was, however, something of
a virtue in their setting, because patrons who linger over
their tea are bad for business. Better to have an abbreviated

visit, to see and be seen, and pay and get out before cramp set in.

The Willow commission was followed by further work for Miss Cranston, who had Mackintosh redecorate and furnish her home in 1904. In the following year he received a commission to design a house for Walter Blackie, the Scottish publishing magnate. Hill House, in Helensburgh, is a masterpiece of domestic architecture, and one of the highpoints of Mackintosh's oeuvre, an astonishing place to experience, one of those architectural wonders that makes one gasp with surprise and pleasure. But its charms are quite unlike those of Frank Lloyd Wright's masterpiece Fallingwater, that extraordinarily sculptural house set perfectly into its landscape. The genius of Hill House, though its exterior has a pleasing Scottish rusticity, is to be found in its interiors, fittings and decoration: 'Here is a house.' said its proud architect. 'It is not an Italian villa, or an English mansion house, a Swiss chalet or a Scotch castle. It is a dwelling house.'

Whereas you imagine that the Kaufmann family, who commissioned Fallingwater, had to adapt to living in it – and what a pleasure to do so! – the Blackies had no such period of adjustment. Hill House was bespoke; it was made to fit them. Its architect initiated the project by spending many days living with the family, observing not merely what they thought they might want, but how they actually lived. He then designed the interiors first, and the external elevation of the building evolved as an organic consequence of what was to go on within. The placement and shape of the windows, for instance, which conventionally precedes a consideration of the inner spaces, are here a reflection of them, and what may have been lost in external symmetry is gained in internal coherence.

The rooms are largely painted white, following the Mackintoshes' paint scheme in the decorations of their own flat, which were so exacting and coordinated that one imagines the vegetables had to be interviewed before appearing at the table. The vogue for white rooms – William Morris used internal whites at Kelmscott Manor in the early 1870s, as did Oscar Wilde in refurbishing his home at 34 Tite Street in London in 1884 – was a distinct rebellion from the fusty browns and dark greens of the Victorian era, and became central to the modernist aesthetic.

Like Wright, Mackintosh demanded total control of the furnishing and fittings of his architectural creations, but unlike Wright, he got it. (Mrs Kaufmann insisted on placing a hideous antique Spanish dining table and chairs by the natural rock outcropping that entered the living room as a fireplace at Fallingwater, which must have made Wright cringe. But, Mrs Kaufmann insisted, it was *her* house.)

Hill House was the Blackies' house, too, but they had perfect confidence in their architect, and were delighted by the choices he made after consultation with them. Thus, the publisher wanted his library directly off the entrance hall, so that he could meet business contacts without disturbing the ongoing life of the house. So, too, the children's room had an alcove with a raised floor, ideal for playing games. (And, as children are noisy, Blackie had requested a master bedroom at the furthest distance from their rooms.) The owner was delighted by the results:

To the larder, kitchen, laundry, etc. he gave minute

attention to fit them for practical needs, and always pleasingly designed. With him the practical came first. The
pleasing design followed of itself ... Every detail, inside
as well as outside, received his careful, I might say loving,
attention ... During the planning and building of Hill
House I necessarily saw much of Mackintosh and could
not but recognise, with wonder, the inexhaustible fertility
in design and astonishing powers of work. Withal, he was
a man of practical competency, satisfactory to deal with in
every way, and of a most likeable nature.

It sounds almost like a letter of reference, and who could
imagine one better? Mackintosh was only thirty-seven, at
the apex of his powers, recognised as one of the best architects in Europe, yet Hill House was to be the last of his
large-scale commissions. Perhaps he was too modern, too
insistent on control of 'total design' – which meant 'leave
all of it to me!' – to gain much more work. In a lecture in
1893 he had insisted that architects and designers be given
greater freedom and independence, but he didn't realise
how few potential patrons would allow such license. Rich
people don't much like being told what to do, particularly
by someone whose taste is better than theirs.

He was admired by a coterie in Scotland, but his real fame
was garnered abroad. In 1900 he was one of the stars of
the 8th Vienna Secession, and also showed at exhibitions
in Moscow and Turin. In 1902 the leading German critic
Hermann Muthesius described him as 'among the first'
creative geniuses of modern architecture. While in Europe
this genius was celebrated, at home his career was founder-
ing. Sadly his designs for the new cathedral in Liverpool,

submitted in 1902, were rejected in favour of the present unprepossessing design. Mackintosh's would have been an astonishing building.

In 1914 the depressed Mackintosh and Margaret, who had continued to collaborate in his projects, moved to Suffolk, and shortly thereafter to London, in the hope of finding new commissions. He couldn't have chosen a worse time. The First World War was just starting, and building projects were severely curtailed. Though he did some brilliantly original work for a patron in Northampton, Mackintosh had to make his living as a fabric designer, at which he was (of course) extremely accomplished.

But money was tight, and in 1923 the couple moved to Port-Vendres in the south of France, where life was easier, more agreeable and a lot cheaper. Mackintosh devoted himself to painting landscapes and botanical studies in watercolour and (as you might have supposed) was exceptionally gifted at it. Indeed, had he produced nothing but these watercolours, his place in twentieth-century art would have been assured. The best examples of these pictures are now worth half a million pounds, when they very occasionally come on the market. Many can be seen in the wonderful collection of Mackintosh material at the Hunterian Art Gallery in Glasgow. In 1927 the couple returned to England due to Mackintosh's cancer. He was in and out of hospital over the next twelve months, and died at the age of sixty in December 1928.

We are accustomed to asking: what poems might Keats, who died at twenty-five, have written in later life? What compositions could one have expected of a mature Mozart, dead at thirty-five? Their truncated lives are tragic enough, and leave us bereft of the sustained benefits of their genius. Yet what are we to say of poor Charles Rennie Mackintosh? The loss of *his* mature architectural work cannot be attributed to a premature demise; it is due to those who failed to acknowledge and to celebrate him. Culturally, it is our fault. We had in our midst one of the great geniuses of the twentieth century. We could be – we should be – looking at an architectural landscape with dozens of Mackintosh buildings in it. They are not there; we look and do not find them. They are lost.

A number of commissions for private houses were given to the benign and wholly agreeable Edwin Lutyens – certainly a less original architect than Mackintosh – because the English are old-school, and when they build their own houses, they like them in the mock-Tudorish mode of the Arts and Crafts movement. Mullioned windows, some nice beams, sloping tiled roofs, big chimneys sort of thing. Nothing too modern; better to dream of the past, to lust after it. It is no coincidence that Edward Hudson, the founder of *Country Life* magazine in 1897, had several houses designed by Lutyens. I can't imagine he would have contemplated one by poor Charles Rennie Mackintosh.

Hardly anyone did, though they might have. The world as we experience and make it, is a configuration of random unlikelinesses, of almost inexpressible contingency. *That it is as it is* is a miracle of probability beyond imaging, for at every millisecond it could be other than it is, replete with new persons, objects, projects. It's no wonder people find the alternative universes hypothesis so compelling. Late Mozart symphonies? Byron's *Memoirs*? Houses by Charles Rennie Mackintosh? In our dreams, and garden sheds.

Afterword

Works of art and literature engage us in profound and unexpected ways, and when those works are torn from us – for it can feel like an act of violence – we are affected in complex and unexpected fashion. Why is that? It has, perhaps, something to do with what art is, and why we value it. Art is not essential to culture; it is culture. Civilisation begins when tribes of apes pause from scratching themselves and hitting each other with sticks and begin to tell and to transmit stories, and to make images. It is a long way, in terms of human development, from eating a pig to drawing a picture of one. Art makes us human. It is how we escape from nature, transcend it and make it ours.

And if art is how we define ourselves as human, it is also how many humans define themselves as individuals. Our taste in the arts, the particular choices and discriminations over which one spends so much time, passion and energy are central to our sense of who we are, and how we wish others to see us.

Something so highly valued carries special attachments, resonates with weighty archetypes. It's no wonder the loss of works of art and literature touches us so deeply, and awakens primordial fears. It is a natural and sympathetic human reflex to dread loss, and to grieve over the ravages of time. How could it not be? We lose our loved ones, our fortunes, our youth, our happiness, our lives. Losing is the opposite of having. Loss is bad. *We must hold on to what we have*.

It is the most understandable, conservative and unrealistic of all human impulses. Yet the experience of loss is central not merely to any human life but to the great cycles of nature, in which the conjoined processes of loss and renewal give us the seasons, the flowers, the sustenance of field and orchard. To be without loss is to be without change, and it is almost impossible to imagine the ennui of a world fixed in place, immutable. To encounter a concept that dull, you have to look at the idea of Heaven, and shiver with apprehension lest you end up there, stuck for ever on that cloud, in a state from which mutability is exiled.

Ultimately the loss of one thing betokens the loss of all. The loss of a great work of art reminds us of the evanescence of objects, and the empty silences to come. We talk of the 'eternal' verities and the 'immortal' Shakespeare as if to shield us from such knowledge, as Keats seems to do in suggesting that his Grecian Urn will speak to the coming generations, as if for ever. Shelley knew better: not merely has Ozymandias, King of Kings, fallen, but the statue of him has toppled as well:

Nothing beside remains. Round the decay
Of that colossal wreck, boundless and bare
The lone and level sands stretch far away.

Art, like life, is inevitably lost. What remains are the forces of obliteration. Every work of art carries the certainty of its loss as an essential aspect of its nature, which makes its place in our world fragile and contingent. Shelley puts this baldly: 'Nought may endure but Mutability.' We have the gift of life, and of art, for a time, and no more. An Epicurean philosopher or an Omar Khayyam would counsel us to delight in them while we may.

So when we hear the words of Amin Maalouf's Astaghfirullah, in the novel *Leo the African*, we should draw strength and consolation from their implacable wisdom:

> Too often, at funerals, I hear men and women believers cursing death. But death is a gift from the Most High, and one cannot curse that which comes from Him. Does the word 'gift' seem incongruous to you? It is nevertheless the absolute truth ... Yes my brothers, let us thank God for having made us this gift of death, so that life is to have meaning; silence, that speech is to have meaning; illness, that health is to have meaning; war, that peace is to have meaning. Let us give thanks to Him for having given us weariness and pain, so that rest and joy are to have meaning. That is, let us celebrate loss, so that presence is to have meaning.

Acknowledgements

A version of Chapter 4 was previously published in *Granta*. Bits and pieces from my online blog 'Finger on the Page' in the *Guardian* will have found their way into a few chapters of this text. Chapters 1, 3, 4, 7, 10–13 and 15 were originally produced, in much shorter and rather different form, for two series of *Lost, Stolen or Shredded* that were aired on BBC Radio 4. The original broadcasts may be heard on my web site: www.gekoski.com. I am deeply grateful to the following, who have read all or some sections of the text with great friendliness: Gretchen Albrecht, Anna Francesca Camilleri, Erika Congreve, Nicholas Garnham, Anna Gekoski, Dame Jenny Gibbs, Ruth Greenberg, Peter Grogan, Mary Kisler, Andrew McGeachin, Robin Muller, John Murray, Stephen Roe, Tom Rosenthal, Jamie Ross, Peter Selley, Rob Shepherd, Anthony Thwaite and (as ever) Sam Varnedoe.

Without my friend and literary agent Peter Straus, Peter Carson and Andrew Franklin this book would not have happened. Sadly, Peter Carson died some months before this book was published. He was a man of remarkable and acute reading, a percipient and encouraging editor, always lively and amusing company. One of the great pleasures of having joined Profile was that I could be edited by a person of such quality, and I will miss him very much. I am also most grateful to Penny Daniel and Cecily Gayford, who have seen the manuscript through the press so efficiently. My research assistant, Elinor Brown, cannot be praised too highly, so I won't even try. My wife, Belinda Kitchin, makes all of this possible, and I am a lot more than grateful to her.

Illustration Credits

While every effort has been made to contact copyright-holders of illustrations, the author and publishers would be grateful for information about any illustrations where they have been unable to trace them, and would be glad to make amendments in further editions.

Index

Figures in *italics* indicate captions.

A

Achebe, Chinua 227–228, 229
Adams, John Quincy 77
Adler, Guido
  death 186–7
  decides not to flee from
    Austria 185–6
  as the first musicologist 185
  his library 184, 186–87, 188,
    189
  Mahler's gift 182–94, 186,
    189–90, 191–2
  'precious relic' from Liszt 184
  retirement from University of
    Vienna 185
  victimised as a Jew 185–6
  'The Scope, Method and
    Goals of Musicology' 185
Adler, Melanie 186–88
Adler, Tom 189–93
Admiralty 46, 47
Aeschylus 207, 208
Africa
  African art 232–3

Arab slave traders 226, 227
Conrad's views 228, 229, 231
'dark continent' 230, 231, 242
'friends' of Africa 230
in the public imagination 231
Saharan vs sub-Saharan 225,
  234
stripped of its cultural and
  artistic heritage 239
thriving set of urban cultures
  in sub-Saharan Africa 241
treated as a single entity
  225–6
Al Qaeda 32, 214
Alexander the Great 201–2
Alexandria 201–2, 207
  library 201, 202, 203, 206–7
  siege of (48 BC) 203
Althorp, Northamptonshire 17
Alvarez, Al 153
American Antiquarian Society,
  Worcester, Massachusetts 83,
  84–5
American League 59
Amis, Kingsley 113, 131
Amis, Martin 115
Amundsen, Roald 172